Contents

Page

Tables

vi

Chapter 1 Introduction

This book is a sister publication to *Young People's Knowledge of Higher Education*. That report, published in 1990, attempted to measure sixth-formers' understanding of higher education, with a view to identifying deficiencies and proposing corrective action.

When *Young People's Knowledge* (YPK) first appeared, some commentators argued that interesting though the findings might be, a more important task was to understand the state of knowledge amongst potential *non-traditional* applicants. Young people in sixth-forms, they argued, were relatively well understood. Higher education also had considerable experience of addressing sixth-formers and their equivalent in colleges of further education, and had developed sophisticated lines of communication. Communications with the potential mature student, on the other hand, were remarkably limited.

This seemed to the authors a reasonable stance. It might have been wrong to assume that young people's knowledge was well understood, but it was certainly right to assume that the knowledge of potential mature students was understood less. There was every possibility that potential mature students harboured important misconceptions about higher education. Perhaps the majority thought that higher education had no interest in them, and would turn them away in the absence of three good A-levels? Perhaps they believed that mature students lacked the sharpness of recent school-leavers, and would have great difficulty in coping with coursework? Perhaps many thought that student grants were exclusively available to recent school-leavers, and that a return to study was therefore financially impossible?

In the absence of systematic informational programmes to overcome the misassumptions that might arise, it remained possible that a large number of potential mature students were permanently lost to higher education. It remained equally possible that misassumptions were distorting the behaviour of those that *did* apply.

The present study was thus planned to provide an objective measurement of the state of knowledge, amongst potential mature students, of higher education. It was expected that this measurement would lead on to conclusions about the most suitable informational programmes to correct the problems highlighted. As with YPK, it was expected that some additional insights would be gathered along the way which would

1

help higher education to communicate more effectively with one of its most important target audiences.

The questionnaire used was, so far as possible, similar to that utilized in YPK: this would allow comparisons to be made between adults and young people. Not all questions were repeated, however, partly because of the different interests of young people and adults, and partly because of what had been learned from *Young People's Knowledge*. It had already been found, for example, that ignorance of validation was profound—there was little point in revisiting this issue. Adults are also far more likely to be interested in part-time courses than traditional students, and so the number of questions on this issue was increased. Again, some questions relevant only to mature students needed to be added—for instance, questions on the rarity or otherwise of mature people in higher education, and on the relative performance of mature students.

Target Audiences

Potential 'traditional' students are very easy to identify: virtually all can be contacted directly via schools and colleges. The situation is much more complex with potential mature students. Two categories of potential mature students, however, could be addressed fairly easily: these were current Access course students, and current mature applicants.

The Access students were thus contacted via correspondence with Access course tutors. Mature applicants were contacted directly, chosen on a random basis from those who had applied through both UCCA and PCAS.

Contacting other potential mature students was significantly more problematic. All adults could be considered potential mature students, but interest would be greater in the younger age ranges and in people from the social and economic backgrounds that had, traditionally, been the more frequent users of higher education.

The approach finally chosen, partly for reasons of practicability and cost, was to contact two groups of adults *through* traditional applicants. A selection of those who had applied through both UCCA and PCAS were asked to contact relatives or friends of the family[1] in the age range

---

[1] For brevity, this category is referred to in the following report as 'Friends', though relatives could have been involved.

25[2]–35. Others who had applied through both clearing houses were asked to seek co-operation from their parents, the great majority of whom would be in the age range 35–55.

This selection process allowed the questionnaire to be targeted, first, on the age ranges of those more likely to be interested in a return to study. Secondly, through their association with the traditional applicant, the majority of those adults approached could be expected to be members of the social and economic groups with greatest traditional involvement in higher education.

Response Rates

The authors had planned (and budgeted) for the analysis of responses from 4,000 adults, preferably divided equally between the four groups. It was expected that response rates would be roughly as follows:

Table 1.1: Expected Participation Rates

Group	Participation	Group	Participation
Parents	25.0%	Access	33.3%
Applicants	33.3%	Friends	20.0%

As a result, 3,000 questionnaires were distributed for completion by both Access students and Applicants, 4,000 were distributed for completion by Parents, and 5,000 for completion by Friends.

The response rate was in fact as follows:

Table 1.2: Actual Participation Rates

Group	Participation	Group	Participation
Parents	1548 (38.7%)	Access	1392 (46.4%)
Applicants	1572 (52.4%)	Friends	679 (13.6%)

As can be seen, response rates exceeded expectations for three of the four categories. Applicants proved the most co-operative of the four adult groups, while Friends were the least likely to take part. The low participation rate of Friends might have been due to sixth-formers having difficulty in identifying appropriate individuals, or a result of the

[2] The definition of 'mature student' used in this study was the traditional '25 or over'. Though higher education institutions often refer to those aged 21 or over as mature for qualification purposes, it was felt that the younger adults might be insufficiently differentiated from recent school leavers for the purpose of this survey.

more limited interest of such individuals in taking part. Though it had been carefully explained to all involved that participating in the research survey would have no effect whatever on PCAS or UCCA applications, it is arguable that Applicants, Parents, and Access students would have greater interest than Friends in retaining cordial relationships with the clearing houses. Strangely enough, the average participation, at 34.6%, was identical—to the first decimal place—to the average participation of sixth-formers.

Since a budget for analysis of 4,000 questionnaires had been set, the numbers of questionnaires finally processed were as follows:

Table 1.3: Responses Analysed

Group	Analysed	Group	Analysed
Parents	1107	Access	1107
Applicants	1107	Friends	679

Survey Period

All questionnaires were distributed in September 1990, for return within one month. Any questionnaires received after that time frame were discarded, and were not included in the above 'return rate' statistics.

In considering the results of the questionnaire, it is important to keep the survey period in mind—a number of changes to higher education, such as changes to institutional titles, occurred just after the survey had been completed.

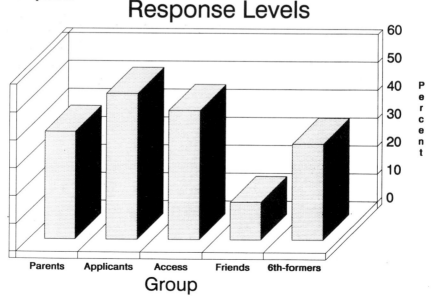

Chapter 2   Knowledge of the Different Types of HE Institutions

Numbers of HEIs

The first set of questions covered adults' knowledge about the numbers of British higher education institutions in each of the three categories—university, polytechnic, and college of higher education. This provided one easily quantifiable indicator of the relative degree of knowledge of higher education among the different groups.

Young People's Knowledge had already shown that a considerable overestimate of numbers could be expected. The average sixth-former had thought there to be 81 universities (the correct number is usually put at 45[3]), 100 polytechnics (as against a correct 30 or 32 at the time of the survey[4]), and 202 CHEs (as against a 'correct' 55—60[5]). Adults made even more flamboyant estimates. The average adult in the survey thought there to be 96 universities, 130 polytechnics, and 227 CHEs. These figures were in fact very close to the estimates made by sixth-formers at the beginning of their sixth-form studies, before they had received specific instruction about higher education: the comparable figures were 97, 139, and 292. It can be safely concluded, therefore, that all groups likely to have an interest in entering higher education significantly overestimate the number of HEIs in Britain.

The overestimate, as noted, did not come as a surprise: what did cause the researchers surprise was the major difference in the knowledge of higher education evinced by the four different adult groups. **Table 2.2**, for instance, indicates the 'sound' and 'unsound' answers of the different groups regarding numbers of universities. Any estimates in the range 40—80 were considered 'sound', but estimates of 200 and above

[3] The specific number given depends on the method of classification, and particularly on whether University of London and University of Wales colleges are counted separately.

[4] During the survey, the number of polytechnics was being raised from 30 to 32. At the time of writing, the number had been increased to 34.

[5] There is no authoritative definition of 'college of higher education', but the term has come to be applied essentially to the colleges represented by the Standing Conference of Principals, since the great bulk of higher education provision outside the universities and polytechnics is provided by this group. If, however, 'college of higher education' is defined as any institution outside the polytechnics and universities which offers, as the majority of its provision, full-time degree and HND work, there is a limited number of additional colleges that could lay claim to the title.

were considered 'unsound'. On this basis, Parents proved to make the best estimates, with just 10.2% of unsound estimates, as against 16.8% of Applicants, who might have been expected to have known more than Parents. Friends did very much worse, with 49.7% providing unsound answers. Much the worst estimates, however, were provided by adults on Access courses, 57.3% of whom thought there to be 200 or more universities. More than a quarter of such students, indeed, thought there to be 500 or more universities, which is wildly at variance with reality.

These patterns were followed closely in estimates of the numbers of polytechnics. **Table 2.4** again shows Parents giving the lowest numbers of unsound answers, and Access students the highest. The great overestimate of the numbers of polytechnics given by Access students (the 'average'[6] Access student thought there to be 167 polytechnics) could be considered particularly disappointing in light of the fact that a large number of Access courses are tied to polytechnic entry.

Table 2.6, covering knowledge of the CHEs, shows a slightly different pattern, though in general it confirms the overall patterns discussed above.

Question 1a: *Approximately how many British universities are there?*

Table 2.1: Numbers of Universities

No of Unis	Parents	Applicants	Access	Friends	Average
30	17.5%	16.4%	5.7%	7.1%	16.0%
40	27.6%	23.7%	5.5%	5.5%	23.3%
60	20.3%	17.1%	7.7%	10.2%	19.0%
80	12.0%	12.8%	8.6%	11.1%	12.4%
100	11.6%	12.0%	14.0%	15.1%	13.0%
200	5.4%	9.0%	16.8%	16.2%	8.1%
300	3.0%	4.4%	14.7%	12.0%	4.1%
500	1.5%	2.5%	15.4%	12.3%	2.3%
800	0.4%	0.8%	10.5%	9.2%	0.8%
No answer	0.7%	1.3%	1.2%	1.2%	1.1%
Average estimate	80.1 unis	98.6 unis	106.0 unis	102.3 unis	96.2 unis

[6] Since this report is addressed to general readers rather than to statisticians, the term 'average' is used where the statistician would use 'arithmetic mean'. The statistician would point out, correctly, that the average (or arithmetic mean) may in this instance overstate the degree of error, given the nature of the question. Averages nevertheless remain instructive, particularly in comparing the answers given by each group. Mode and median answers are readily derived from the tables given.

Table 2.2: Sound and Unsound Answers—Universities

	Parents	Applicants	Access	Friends	Average
Sound (40–80)	65.5%	57.1%	18.9%	22.8%	58.2%
Unsound (200–800)	10.2%	16.8%	57.3%	49.7%	15.4%

Question 1b: *Approximately how many British polytechnics are there?*

Table 2.3: Numbers of Polytechnics

	Parents	Applicants	Access	Friends	Average
30	10.8%	9.5%	6.0%	6.5%	8.4%
40	15.1%	16.3%	10.7%	11.9%	13.7%
60	21.1%	18.9%	14.5%	18.3%	18.2%
80	15.6%	14.3%	17.3%	16.5%	15.9%
100	16.1%	16.2%	16.4%	19.3%	16.8%
200	11.5%	10.0%	14.7%	12.5%	12.2%
300	5.5%	8.1%	11.0%	8.7%	8.3%
500	2.8%	4.4%	5.9%	3.7%	4.3%
800	0.5%	0.6%	2.2%	1.2%	1.1%
No answer	1.0%	1.5%	1.3%	1.3%	1.3%
Average Estimate	109.3 pols	122.2 pols	156.3 pols	131.0 pols	129.5 pols

Table 2.4: Sound and Unsound Answers—Polytechnics

	Parents	Applicants	Access	Friends	Average
Sound (30–40)	25.9%	25.8%	16.6%	18.4%	22.0%
Unsound (100–800)	36.4%	39.5%	50.2%	45.4%	42.6%

7

Question 1c: *Approximately how many British colleges of higher education are there?*

Table 2.5: Numbers of Colleges of Higher Education

	Parents	Applicants	Access	Friends	Average
30	10.6%	10.5%	5.7%	7.1%	8.6%
40	8.3%	9.0%	5.4%	5.5%	7.2%
60	11.9%	12.3%	7.6%	10.2%	10.5%
80	9.5%	9.7%	8.5%	11.1%	9.5%
100	15.0%	13.4%	13.9%	15.1%	14.3%
200	18.0%	14.6%	16.6%	16.1%	16.3%
300	11.2%	11.0%	14.5%	12.0%	12.2%
500	8.8%	11.1%	15.3%	12.3%	11.8%
800	5.4%	6.1%	10.4%	9.2%	7.7%
No answer	1.4%	2.4%	2.1%	1.6%	1.9%
Average Answer	196.2 CHEs	207.1 CHEs	271.1 CHEs	240.9 CHEs	227.5 CHEs

Table 2.6: Sound and Unsound Answers—Colleges of Higher Education

	Parents	Applicants	Access	Friends	Average
Sound (40–100)	44.7%	44.3%	35.4%	41.8%	41.5%
Unsound (200+)	43.4%	42.9%	56.8%	49.5%	48.0%

Size of Higher Education Institutions

Question 2: *On average, how many full-time students does each of the types of institution have?*

The second set of questions concerned the size of higher education institutions (HEIs). Again, this provides an easily quantifiable indicator of the relative degree of knowledge of higher education, and gives clues as to how the different types of HEI are perceived.

Table 2.7 shows that all adult groups significantly underestimated, on average, the size of universities, though they gave slightly higher estimates than sixth-formers, whose average estimate had been 3,981.

(The actual average size of universities during this survey period was approximately 5,600.) **Table 2.8** shows that adult groups also underestimated the size of polytechnics, but this time they gave significantly better estimates than sixth-formers (sixth-form average: 3,467). The adult estimates of the size of CHEs, however, was less accurate than that of the sixth-formers (sixth-form average: 2,603), overestimating their size to an even greater extent. Adults, even more than sixth-formers, failed to appreciate one of the major differentiating features of the CHE sector: the colleges' much smaller scale. (The average CHE, during the period of this survey, had fewer than 1,500 full-time students.)

Table 2.7: Average Size of Universities

Size	Parents	Applicants	Access	Friends	Average
1,000	7.6%	5.8%	11.7%	5.8%	7.9%
2,000	15.9%	18.2%	23.2%	16.7%	18.7%
3,000	21.3%	23.0%	23.6%	25.7%	23.2%
4,000	22.7%	24.4%	20.5%	19.6%	22.1%
6,000	20.9%	17.2%	12.6%	21.2%	17.6%
8,000	10.3%	9.8%	7.0%	10.0%	9.2%
No answer	1.3%	1.6%	1.4%	1.0%	1.4%
Average	4,130	4,050	3,560	4,120	3,950

Table 2.8: Average Size of Polytechnics

	Parents	Applicants	Access	Friends	Average
1,000	4.4%	3.7%	6.3%	4.9%	4.8%
2,000	22.0%	18.4%	25.4%	20.2%	21.7%
3,000	24.6%	25.0%	28.2%	23.2%	25.5%
4,000	23.9%	25.0%	20.6%	25.8%	23.6%
6,000	17.3%	20.0%	13.6%	16.8%	17.0%
8,000	6.3%	6.3%	4.3%	8.1%	6.1%
No answer	1.4%	1.5%	1.5%	1.0%	1.4%
Average	3,850	4,000	3,540	3,930	3,820

Table 2.9: Average Size of Colleges of Higher Education

	Parents	Applicants	Access	Friends	Average
1,000	33.2%	25.9%	23.8%	30.1%	4.8%
2,000	32.9%	31.7%	29.1%	29.2%	21.7%
3,000	14.0%	18.8%	18.3%	15.9%	25.5%
4,000	9.7%	11.0%	12.4%	7.8%	23.6%
6,000	4.8%	5.4%	8.6%	8.8%	16.9%
8,000	4.5%	5.2%	6.6%	7.2%	6.1%
No answer	1.0%	1.9%	1.2%	0.9%	1.4%
Average	2,530	2,820	3,010	2,860	2,800

The following table summarises the percentage of sound answers given by each adult group to the questions concerning HEI size. It can be seen that Parents proved to give the most accurate answers overall to questions on the sizes of HEIs, but not by a substantial margin, because they were outperformed by Applicants and Friends on the size of polytechnics. The table shows very clearly, however, that Access students gave the least accurate answers to all three questions, and by a substantial margin.

Table 2.10: Synopsis of Sound Answers on Size of HEIs

	Parents	Applicants	Access	Friends	Total
Unis	43.7%	41.6%	33.1%	40.9%	39.7%
Polys	41.2%	45.0%	34.2%	42.6%	40.6%
CHEs	66.1%	57.6%	52.9%	59.3%	58.9%
Average	50.3%	48.0%	40.1%	47.6%	46.4%

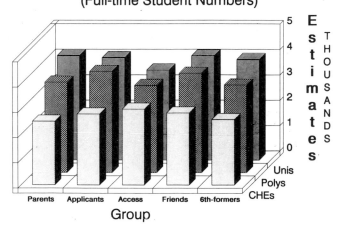

Estimates of Size of HEIs
(Full-time Student Numbers)

Chapter 3   Knowledge of Grants

A series of three questions on grants was included, essentially, to check on whether adults thought awards to be available only to recent school-leavers. Clearly such an assumption would adversely affect interest in applying for higher education places.

Mandatory Awards for Full-time Study

Question 3: *Is a student grant automatically available (assuming you are British, have not previously received a grant, etc) to mature students for full-time degree courses in: [universities, polytechnics, and CHEs].*

The synoptic **Table 3.4** shows that adults were fairly evenly divided on whether mandatory awards were available to mature students. A small majority of Parents and Friends thought they would not be available, while an even smaller majority of Access students thought they *would* be. Only the Applicant group displayed any confidence in the availability of such grants.

Tables 3.1 to 3.3—indeed all tables on grants—make it clear that adults, like sixth-formers, believe that grants chase types of institution, rather than types of course. This is made most evident by the answers given to the question on CHEs. Parents, for instance, were fairly evenly divided on availability of grants at universities, but were more likely to accept their non-availability at polytechnics, and much more likely to accept their non-availability at CHEs. This pattern—of thinking that grants were most likely to be available for degree courses at universities, and least likely to be available at CHEs, was common to all adult and sixth-form groups. It is significant that Access students were, as a group, reasonably sure that grants were available for university and polytechnic degree courses, but even more sure that they would *not* be available at a CHE.

It might be concluded that CHEs would be wise to promote the fact that the same rules on grants apply to them as to universities and polytechnics. However, the greater problem no doubt lies in the failure amongst many adults to differentiate between colleges of *higher* education and colleges of *further* education. Thus, there would be more utility in an informational programme indicating that grants followed types of course rather than types of institution.

11

Table 3.1: Availability of Mandatory Awards for Full-time Degrees in Universities

	Parents	Applicants	Access	Friends	Average
Yes	48.6%	68.6%	59.2%	51.3%	57.5%
No	50.4%	30.7%	40.3%	48.1%	41.8%
No answer	1.0%	0.7%	0.5%	0.6%	0.8%

Table 3.2: Availability of Mandatory Awards for Full-time Degrees in Polytechnics

	Parents	Applicants	Access	Friends	Average
Yes	47.6%	66.6%	58.2%	48.4%	55.9%
No	51.4%	32.6%	40.9%	51.0%	43.2%
No answer	1.0%	0.8%	0.9%	0.6%	0.9%

Table 3.3: Availability of Mandatory Awards for Full-time Degrees in CHEs

	Parents	Applicants	Access	Friends	Average
Yes	38.8%	51.1%	39.2%	32.9%	41.3%
No	60.3%	48.0%	59.9%	66.4%	57.8%
No answer	1.0%	0.9%	0.9%	0.7%	0.9%

Table 3.4 (Synoptic): Availability of Mandatory Awards for Full-time Degrees in HEIs

	Parents	Applicants	Access	Friends	Average
Yes	45.0%	62.1%	52.2%	44.2%	51.6%
No	54.0%	37.1%	47.0%	55.2%	47.6%
No answer	1.0%	0.8%	0.8%	0.6%	0.9%

Discretionary Awards for Full-time Study

Question 4: *Is a DISCRETIONARY student grant available (i.e. if your local authority so chooses) to mature students for full-time degree courses in: [universities, polytechnics and colleges of higher education].*

Tables 3.5 to 3.8 show that adults were fairly well convinced that discretionary assistance for full-time degree study was available, with Parents most convinced of it, and Access students least convinced. Curiously, adults were most likely to associate discretionary awards with polytechnics, and least likely with CHEs.

Table 3.5: Availability of Discretionary Awards for Full-time Degrees in Universities

	Parents	Applicants	Access	Friends	Average
Yes	88.3%	81.6%	78.5%	84.4%	83.1%
No	10.8%	17.3%	20.1%	14.5%	15.8%
No answer	0.8%	1.2%	1.4%	1.2%	1.2%

Table 3.6: Availability of Discretionary Awards for Full-time Degrees in Polytechnics

	Parents	Applicants	Access	Friends	Average
Yes	88.7%	82.6%	82.4%	84.4%	84.5%
No	10.3%	16.3%	16.1%	14.5%	14.3%
No answer	1.0%	1.2%	1.5%	1.2%	1.2%

Table 3.7: Availability of Discretionary Awards for Full-time Degrees in CHEs

	Parents	Applicants	Access	Friends	Average
Yes	81.5%	75.9%	77.1%	76.7%	77.9%
No	17.5%	23.0%	21.4%	22.0%	20.9%
No answer	1.0%	1.1%	1.5%	1.3%	1.3%

Table 3.8 (Synoptic): Availability of Discretionary Awards for Full-time Degrees in HEIs

	Parents	Applicants	Access	Friends	Average
Yes	86.2%	80.0%	79.3%	81.9%	81.9%
No	12.9%	18.8%	19.2%	17.0%	17.0%
No answer	0.9%	1.1%	1.5%	1.1%	1.1%

Discretionary Awards for Part-time Study

Question 4: *Is a discretionary student grant available (i.e. if your local authority so chooses) to mature students for PART-TIME degree courses in: [universities, polytechnics and colleges of higher education].*

Tables 3.9 to 3.12 indicate that adults do not, as a whole, have a clear view on whether grants are or are not available for part-time study. On the whole, they tend to the view that such grants are not available, though they are slightly more inclined to believe that grants are available in polytechnics than in other HEIs.

Table 3.9: Availability of Discretionary Grants for Part-time Degrees in Universities

	Parents	Applicants	Access	Friends	Average
Yes	47.6%	43.5%	42.2%	41.2%	43.9%
No	51.2%	53.5%	55.9%	56.9%	54.1%
No answer	1.3%	3.1%	1.9%	2.1%	2.1%

Table 3.10: Availability of Discretionary Grants for Part-time Degrees in Polytechnics

	Parents	Applicants	Access	Friends	Average
Yes	50.6%	44.0%	42.0%	42.9%	45.1%
No	48.1%	53.0%	56.2%	55.5%	53.0%
No answer	1.3%	3.0%	1.8%	1.6%	2.0%

Table 3.11: Availability of Discretionary Grants for Part-time Degrees in CHEs

	Parents	Applicants	Access	Friends	Average
Yes	46.8%	41.1%	39.6%	39.7%	42.0%
No	51.9%	55.8%	58.8%	58.4%	56.0%
No answer	1.3%	3.1%	1.6%	1.6%	2.0%

Table 3.12 (Synoptic): Availability of Discretionary Grants for Part-time Degrees in HEIs

	Parents	Applicants	Access	Friends	Average
Yes	48.3%	42.8%	41.3%	41.2%	43.6%
No	50.4%	54.1%	56.9%	56.9%	54.3%
No answer	1.3%	3.0%	1.8%	1.9%	2.0%

Summary

The following table summarises the 'yes' answers to questions on availability of grants. The rules regarding grants are quite complex, with a number of codicils, but it remains reasonable to call this table a summary of 'correct' answers.

The table makes it clear that adults are confident only in the availability of discretionary grants for full-time courses. There is very little confidence that any other type of grant is available, and this could indeed materially affect the interest of adults in entering higher education.

Table 3.13: Summary of 'Yes' Answers on Grants

	Parents	Applicants	Access	Friends	Average
F-T mandatory	45.0%	62.1%	52.2%	44.2%	51.6%
F-T discretionary	86.2%	80.0%	79.3%	81.9%	91.9%
P-T discretionary	48.3%	42.8%	41.3%	41.2%	43.6%
Average	59.8%	61.6%	57.6%	55.8%	59.0%

Mature Student Grants
"Correct" Answers

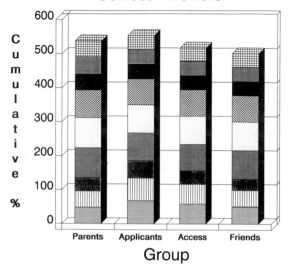

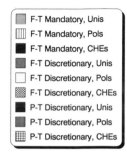

F-T Mandatory, Unis
F-T Mandatory, Pols
F-T Mandatory, CHEs
F-T Discretionary, Unis
F-T Discretionary, Pols
F-T Discretionary, CHEs
P-T Discretionary, Unis
P-T Discretionary, Pols
P-T Discretionary, CHEs

Group

Chapter 4 Knowledge of Courses Available

Length of Courses: Full-time

Question 6: *What is the normal length of the following courses in England and Wales if taken on a full-time basis?*

Table 4.1: Length of Full-time Study for Ordinary Degree

	Parents	Applicants	Access	Friends	Total
1 year	0.4%	0.5%	3.3%	2.5%	1.6%
2 years	5.4%	6.6%	12.8%	11.1%	8.7%
3 years	92.1%	90.4%	77.1%	82.3%	85.8%
4 years	1.8%	2.2%	5.3%	3.2%	3.3%
5 years	0.0%	0.0%	0.3%	0.3%	0.1%
6 years	0.0%	0.0%	0.0%	0.0%	0.0%
No answer	0.4%	0.3%	1.1%	0.6%	0.6%
Average	2.96 years	2.94 years	2.86 years	2.88 years	2.91 years

On average, the adults gave slightly better answers to this question than sixth-formers, 84.7% of whom gave the 'correct' answer of three years. Parents performed particularly well—even better than sixth-formers at their most knowledgable phase[7] and very much better than Access students, almost a quarter of whom gave wrong answers.

Table 4.2: Length of Full-time Study for Honours Degree

	Parents	Applicants	Access	Friends	Total
1 year	0.1%	0.2%	0.9%	1.2%	0.5%
2 years	0.3%	0.7%	3.0%	1.9%	1.4%
3 years	64.5%	64.4%	36.2%	50.7%	54.3%
4 years	32.4%	32.6%	52.3%	41.0%	39.4%
5 years	2.0%	1.5%	5.1%	3.8%	3.0%
6 years	0.3%	0.2%	1.4%	1.0%	0.7%
No answer	0.4%	0.4%	1.0%	0.3%	0.5%
Average	3.37 years	3.35 years	3.63 years	3.48 years	3.40 years

[7] Sixth-formers were surveyed at four different stages of the sixth-form cycle: at the start of the lower sixth; at the end of the lower sixth; in December of the upper sixth; and March of the upper sixth. In general, they gave the most accurate answers during the third phase—December of the upper sixth.

ises to this question were very similar, overall, to those published ̤̤. ̤̤̤̤ng *People's Knowledge*: in both cases, a substantial minority made the erroneous assumption that English and Welsh honours degrees typically required an extra year of study over ordinary degrees. Access students, however, were particularly weak on this question, with only 36.2% giving the correct answer to one of the most basic questions about the whole of higher education. Yet again, Parents outperformed sixth-formers at their most knowledgable phase (62.1%), but this time they were joined in their success by the adult Applicants.

Table 4.3: Length of Full-time Study for HND

	Parents	Applicants	Access	Friends	Total
1 year	2.9%	4.2%	4.2%	4.9%	4.0%
2 years	68.7%	73.3%	51.5%	62.5%	64.2%
3 years	20.7%	14.5%	19.2%	20.2%	18.5%
4 years	5.9%	5.3%	11.7%	7.5%	7.6%
5 years	0.4%	1.4%	7.7%	3.1%	3.2%
6 years	0.5%	0.5%	3.2%	1.3%	1.4%
No answer	0.9%	0.8%	2.0%	0.4%	1.1%
Average	2.33 years	2.28 years	2.76 years	2.45 years	2.35 years

Adults as a whole performed remarkably well on this question, with 64.2% giving the correct answer, compared with 53.2% of sixth-formers. The answers would have been even more impressive were it not for the weakness of Access students, whose answers were both more inaccurate, and with a wider scattering, than those of sixth-formers. The answers would certainly seem to indicate that Access students are not being given a great deal of information about the HND, though the qualification, with its shorter duration, more vocational bent and less competitive entry requirements, might be considered particularly relevant to many Access students. The very high levels of correct answers given by adult Applicants (73.3%) certainly indicates that the award commends itself to many potential mature students.

Length of Courses: Part-time

Question 7: *What is the normal length of the following courses in England and Wales if taken on a part-time basis?*

The length of study for degrees varies much more widely in part-time than full-time mode, but the most popular length is four years for part-time ordinary degrees, and five years for part-time honours degrees. The average responses of adults, indicated in **Tables 4.4 and 4.5** can be seen to be relatively close to this, with limited scattering. Much greater scattering of answers was visible for the HNC, which is clearly much less well understood by adults than the HND.

Table 4.4: Length of Part-time Study for Ordinary Degree

	Parents	Applicants	Access	Friends	Total
2 years	1.7%	2.0%	6.0%	5.5%	3.6%
3 years	11.5%	8.8%	14.2%	13.0%	11.8%
4 years	43.0%	39.8%	35.0%	42.8%	39.9%
5 years	32.0%	31.6%	26.7%	27.4%	29.7%
6 years	9.3%	14.9%	13.5%	9.7%	12.1%
7 years	0.3%	1.2%	1.3%	0.6%	0.8%
No answer	2.1%	1.4%	2.7%	0.9%	1.9%
Average	4.38 years	4.54 years	4.34 years	4.26 years	4.39 years

Table 4.5: Normal Length of Study for Part-time Honours Degree

	Parents	Applicants	Access	Friends	Total
2 year	0.5%	0.8%	1.4%	1.9%	1.1%
3 years	4.2%	4.2%	6.5%	5.9%	5.1%
4 years	27.0%	23.8%	19.8%	23.6%	23.5%
5 years	40.9%	38.4%	32.8%	37.5%	37.4%
6 years	17.5%	22.1%	21.6%	20.8%	20.5%
7 years	4.3%	4.7%	7.9%	5.3%	5.6%
8 years	3.4%	4.2%	7.0%	4.0%	4.7%
No answer	2.1%	1.7%	3.0%	1.0%	2.0%
Average	4.99 years	5.10 years	5.22 years	5.22 years	5.09 years

Table 4.6: Normal Length of Study for Part-Time HNC

	Parents	Applicants	Access	Friends	Total
2 years	21.3%	22.9%	15.9%	22.1%	20.4%
3 years	37.4%	38.7%	29.9%	36.3%	35.5%
4 years	26.1%	22.7%	24.5%	23.4%	24.2%
5 years	9.2%	7.4%	9.9%	8.3%	8.7%
6 years	3.3%	3.8%	7.6%	4.7%	4.9%
7 years	0.2%	0.8%	4.9%	1.9%	1.9%
8 years	0.4%	1.1%	3.7%	2.2%	1.8%
No answer	2.1%	2.5%	3.6%	1.0%	2.4%
Average	3.36 years	3.35 years	3.93 years	3.51 years	3.54 years

Table 4.7: Summary of Sound Answers

	Parents	Applicants	Access	Friends	Total
Ordinary (3−5)	86.5%	80.3%	76.0%	83.2%	81.3%
Honours (4−6)	85.4%	84.3%	74.2%	81.9%	81.4%
HNC (2−3)	58.7%	61.7%	45.8%	58.4%	55.9%
Average	76.9%	75.4%	65.3%	74.5%	72.9%

Knowledge of Courses Available

Question 8: *Are degrees available in each of the following subjects at each type of institution?*

Degrees were in fact available in all subjects at each type of institution, with the exceptions of Medicine, which was available only in the university sector, and Secretarial Studies, which was not available in that sector.

Table 4.8: Availability of Degrees in Medicine

	Universities			Polytechnics			CHEs		
	Yes	No	0	Yes	No	0	Yes	No	0
Parents	98.0%	1.5%	0.5%	14.0%	85.1%	0.9%	1.8%	97.0%	1.2%
Applicants	95.4%	3.4%	1.2%	24.6%	73.2%	2.2%	5.0%	92.8%	2.2%
Access	95.8%	2.4%	1.7%	26.6%	71.1%	2.3%	6.3%	91.3%	2.4%
Friends	97.3%	1.8%	0.9%	22.7%	75.7%	1.6%	4.0%	94.8%	1.2%
Total	96.6%	2.3%	1.1%	21.9%	76.3%	1.8%	4.3%	93.9%	1.8%

The answers for Medicine saw Parents setting the pattern for this series of questions, by providing the most accurate answers of the four adult groups. All adult groups, however, were much clearer than sixth-formers about the non-availability of Medicine in the polytechnic and CHE sectors (sixth-formers gave 'yes' answers of 34.1% and 11.0% respectively).

It is interesting that CHEs were considered to be quite *emphatically* not the type of institutions that would offer degree courses in Medicine.

Table 4.9: Availability of Degrees in Business Studies

	Universities			Polytechnics			CHEs		
	Yes	No	0	Yes	No	0	Yes	No	0
Parents	84.8%	14.3%	0.9%	98.6%	1.1%	0.3%	82.0%	17.3%	0.7%
Applicants	76.8%	21.8%	1.4%	97.5%	1.4%	1.2%	85.0%	13.6%	1.5%
Access	70.2%	27.4%	2.4%	93.6%	4.1%	2.3%	75.8%	21.9%	2.3%
Friends	79.8%	19.0%	1.2%	97.1%	2.2%	0.7%	84.1%	15.0%	0.9%
Total	77.7%	20.8%	1.5%	96.6%	2.2%	1.2%	81.4%	17.2%	1.4%

Like sixth-formers, adults associated polytechnics more closely with Business Studies than any other subject: only Engineering came close, though that was very definitely in second place. This set of figures, along with those following, indicates that polytechnics are perceived as essentially vocational.

There was much greater hesitation in associating Business Studies with universities, though the subject is in fact quite widely available in the sector. This provides an early indication, confirmed by the answers to the question about the availability of Philosophy, that universities are much more closely associated with 'academic' subjects. Access students, in particular, seem to make that association, with more than a quarter thinking that universities would not offer Business Studies.

Table 4.10: Availability of Degrees in Textile Studies

	Universities			Polytechnics			CHEs		
	Yes	No	0	Yes	No	0	Yes	No	0
Parents	43.0%	55.0%	2.0%	94.3%	5.1%	0.6%	80.3%	18.8%	0.9%
Applicants	44.3%	53.2%	2.4%	91.5%	7.1%	1.4%	77.1%	20.8%	2.2%
Access	44.4%	52.3%	3.2%	87.3%	9.7%	3.0%	64.1%	33.2%	2.7%
Friends	42.8%	55.0%	2.2%	91.0%	8.1%	0.9%	80.8%	18.3%	0.9%
Total	43.7%	53.8%	2.5%	91.1%	7.4%	1.5%	75.0%	23.2%	1.8%

These figures generally reinforce the above conclusion about the polytechnics being seen as the home of the 'applied' subjects, and universities as the home of the 'academic' subjects. There is also evidence of considerable willingness to associate colleges of higher education with the 'practical' subjects; the high score is certainly not based on any solid reality, since Textile Studies is available in only a small number of CHEs.

Table 4.11: Availability of Degrees in Engineering

	Universities			Polytechnics			CHEs		
	Yes	No	0	Yes	No	0	Yes	No	0
Parents	96.2%	3.2%	0.6%	96.8%	2.8%	0.4%	58.0%	41.0%	1.0%
Applicants	89.7%	8.7%	1.6%	95.8%	2.6%	1.5%	65.2%	33.0%	1.8%
Access	82.4%	15.4%	2.2%	91.6%	6.1%	2.3%	59.3%	38.1%	2.6%
Friends	90.9%	8.0%	1.2%	94.1%	5.0%	0.9%	60.9%	37.3%	1.8%
Total	89.7%	8.9%	1.4%	94.7%	4.0%	1.3%	60.9%	37.3%	1.8%

One of the most noticeable features of this table is the considerable divergence between Parents and Access students on the availability of Engineering in universities. Parents, correctly, had very little doubt that it was available. Access students were in much greater doubt: they were almost five times more likely to answer the question incorrectly. This table indicates that Parents' beliefs are less based on stereotypes about universities being the home of 'non-vocational' subjects, and more solidly based on knowledge of what is on offer.

It is noticeable that CHEs were much more closely associated with Textile Studies than Engineering, perhaps because of an 'art college' image, although Engineering is in reality more widely available in the sector.

Table 4.12: Availability of Degrees in Philosophy

	Universities			Polytechnics			CHEs		
	Yes	No	0	Yes	No	0	Yes	No	0
Parents	98.8%	0.7%	0.5%	71.9%	26.9%	1.2%	30.1%	68.4%	1.4%
Applicants	97.6%	1.3%	1.2%	77.6%	21.1%	1.3%	33.9%	64.2%	1.9%
Access	96.1%	1.8%	2.1%	69.5%	27.7%	2.8%	31.6%	64.8%	3.6%
Friends	98.4%	0.9%	0.7%	74.3%	24.5%	1.2%	31.9%	66.4%	1.8%
Total	97.6%	1.2%	1.2%	73.2%	25.2%	1.6%	31.9%	65.9%	2.2%

Amongst adults, as amongst sixth-formers, Philosophy is seen to be the archetypical university subject, with only 1.2% saying that it was not available in the sector. Philosophy was not felt to be particularly alien to the polytechnics, however, showing that they are by no means thought of as purely vocational. By contrast, Philosophy was seen to be distinctly alien to the CHE sector, though it is in fact more commonly taught in this sector than in polytechnics. Again, we can see just how inaccurate is the general view of this sector.

Table 4.13: Availability of Degrees in English

	Universities			Polytechnics			CHEs		
	Yes	No	0	Yes	No	0	Yes	No	0
Parents	98.5%	0.9%	0.6%	85.6%	13.4%	1.0%	64.6%	33.9%	1.5%
Applicants	97.4%	1.3%	1.3%	88.8%	9.7%	1.5%	64.8%	33.2%	2.0%
Access	95.0%	3.1%	1.9%	84.0%	13.4%	2.6%	61.5%	35.1%	3.4%
Friends	96.5%	2.4%	1.2%	88.9%	9.9%	1.2%	65.0%	33.7%	1.2%
Total	96.9%	1.8%	1.3%	86.6%	11.8%	1.6%	63.9%	34.0%	2.1%

This table, unlike the next, yields no particular new insights.

23

Table 4.14: Availability of Degrees in Teacher Training

	Universities			Polytechnics			CHEs		
	Yes	No	0	Yes	No	0	Yes	No	0
Parents	68.5%	30.7%	0.8%	79.0%	20.2%	0.8%	75.1%	24.1%	0.8%
Applicants	68.3%	30.3%	1.4%	83.6%	15.0%	1.4%	67.1%	31.3%	1.6%
Access	70.5%	26.9%	2.6%	76.6%	20.8%	2.6%	52.7%	44.6%	2.7%
Friends	65.2%	33.3%	1.5%	78.0%	21.0%	1.0%	68.6%	30.1%	1.3%
Total	68.4%	29.9%	1.6%	79.4%	19.1%	1.5%	65.5%	32.8%	1.7%

The fact that the CHEs are the sector *least* associated with teacher education—though they could be considered to be the market leader in the sphere, many of them having evolved from, or still being, teacher training monotechnics—again indicates their failure to achieve any widespread understanding amongst the general public. It is particularly distressing that nearly half the Access students believed that CHEs would *not* provide teacher education courses. It is arguable that teacher education courses would be particularly well suited to many Access course students, and thus the failure of such students to recognise the primary providers of such courses should be a cause for real concern.

Table 4.15: Availability of Degrees in Secretarial Studies

	Universities			Polytechnics			CHEs		
	Yes	No	0	Yes	No	0	Yes	No	0
Parents	6.1%	92.5%	1.4%	51.4%	47.8%	1.2%	85.9%	13.4%	0.7%
Applicants	9.6%	88.5%	1.9%	51.6%	46.2%	2.2%	85.0%	13.5%	1.5%
Access	13.6%	82.9%	3.4%	60.9%	36.6%	2.5%	79.5%	18.0%	2.5%
Friends	10.5%	87.6%	1.9%	54.2%	44.6%	1.2%	87.2%	11.9%	0.9%
Total	9.6%	88.2%	2.2%	54.5%	43.7%	1.8%	84.3%	14.2%	1.5%

This table indicates, rather more clearly than any other, that Access students are distinctly out of step with the other adult groups. Perhaps more significantly, though, it must compound the discomfiture of the colleges of higher education: they are seen to be, above all else, providers of secretarial courses. This perception was shared by adults and sixth-formers alike, and makes it abundantly clear that 'colleges of higher education', unlike 'teacher-training colleges', have failed almost completely to transmit an accurate understanding of their nature. Since they are perceived as institutions that emphatically would not teach courses in Medicine; would not be at all likely to teach courses in Philosophy; but would be distinctly likely to teach Textile Studies and extremely likely to teach Secretarial Studies, it is hard to avoid the conclusion that the sector is perceived essentially in terms of being the 'downmarket' element of higher education.

Summary of Answers

The following table summarizes the correct and incorrect answers given by each adult group for each sector.

Table 4.16: Synopsis of Correct & Incorrect Answers

	Universities			Polytechnics			CHEs		
	Right	Wrong	No answ	Right	Wrong	No answ	Right	Wrong	No answ
Parents	85.1%	14.0%	0.9%	82.8%	16.4%	0.8%	71.6%	27.4%	1.0%
Applicants	82.2%	16.2%	1.6%	82.4%	16.0%	1.6%	71.4%	26.8%	1.8%
Access	79.7%	17.9%	2.4%	79.3%	18.1%	2.6%	64.5%	32.7%	2.8%
Friends	82.3%	16.4%	1.3%	81.7%	17.2%	1.1%	71.7%	27.1%	1.2%
Total	82.4%	16.0%	1.6%	81.6%	16.9%	1.5%	69.6%	28.6%	1.8%

Parents, overall, proved the best informed of the adult groups—even better informed than adult Applicants themselves. There is room for Parents to feel some pride in this result, and pride which is reinforced by the fact that they gained a higher score, for universities and polytechnics, than the average sixth-former on these questions. (Sixth-formers' average 'correct' scores were 80.1% for universities, 78.6% for polytechnics, and 73.7% for CHEs.) Extraordinarily, Parents even gained a higher score than those sixth-formers surveyed at the end of their sixth-form studies: scores for sixth-formers at that point were 82.3% for universities, 79.8% for polytechnics, and 75.8% for CHEs.

One explanation of the better performance of Parents than Applicants and sixth-formers is that the latter groups would tend to focus on a particular area, and thus would not gain the broader view acquired by the Parents. The figures remain powerful evidence, nevertheless, that Parents take their responsibilities seriously; they even help support the view that Parents are in many respects the chief 'customers' of higher education, and will thus be the most discerning.

It is equally noticeable that Access students provided the lowest proportion of correct answers overall, for all three types of institution, and by some considerable margin. The Access students' markedly lower scores for CHEs could be considered particularly disappointing, since the colleges, given both their profile of work, their much smaller size, and general educational philosophy, makes them particularly suited to Access students.

Throughout this survey, the answers of Access students conform to the pattern shown above: with few exceptions, they prove significantly less accurate than those of other groups. Two things need to be borne in mind in this context. First, they were being surveyed at the *beginning* of their course, not at the end: the survey thus remains silent on the quality and quantity of information provided by the course itself. Secondly, it is a mistake to assume that all such students are preparing themselves for places in higher education: Chapter 8 will show that large numbers of Access course students are, contrary to popular belief, not at all interested in applying for a place in higher education.

Estimates of Numbers of HEIs

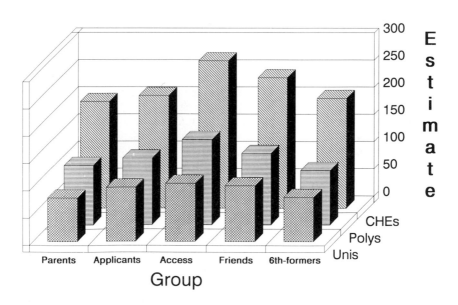

Chapter 5 Knowledge of Entry Requirements

Entry Requirements for a Full-time Degree Course

Question 9: *What, in practice, are the minimum entry requirements for a mature student to enter higher education to study for a FULL-TIME degree?*

Table 5.1: Minimum Requirements to Enter HE for a Full-time Degree

	Parents	Applicants	Access	Friends	Total
No formal Qualifications	26.4%	49.7%	41.5%	29.1%	37.5%
5 O-levels or equivalent	20.1%	15.1%	14.4%	18.6%	16.9%
1 A-level or equivalent	9.8%	9.8%	6.8%	10.5%	9.1%
2 A-levels or equivalent	29.0%	20.4%	27.1%	27.6%	25.8%
3 A-levels or equivalent	14.3%	4.3%	9.5%	14.0%	10.1%
No answer	0.4%	0.7%	0.8%	0.3%	0.6%

Applicants were the most likely to state—correctly—that no formal educational requirements are necessary for mature students. Parents were the least convinced of this, perhaps because their children's experience shows them that the 'price' of entry can be high for traditional students.

It is significant that a majority of adults, in all groups, either did not realize that formal educational requirements could be waived for mature applicants, or felt that they would not be waived in practice. Almost half believed that A-levels or their equivalent remained an essential prerequisite to entry for mature students.

Though this particular question was of course not answered by sixth-formers, their answers to other questions about entry requirements were similar in spirit. Sixth-formers tended to assume that the minimum A-level grades required in practice were those of the more selective institutions. Treating such institutions as the norm is clearly unhelpful to the expansion of access. Mature student access would certainly be facilitated if the perceived norm for entry was based on the requirements of the institutions with most interest in mature entrants, not on the requirements of the institutions with limited interest in them.

Minimum Requirements for a Part-time Degree Course

Question 10: *What, in practice, are the minimum entry requirements for a mature student to enter higher education to study for a* PART-TIME *degree.*

Table 5.2: Minimum Requirements to Enter HE for a Part-time Degree

	Parents	Applicants	Access	Friends	Total
No Qualifications	43.9%	64.9%	54.6%	41.9%	52.3%
5 O-levels	23.1%	12.8%	13.0%	23.9%	17.6%
1 A-level	11.6%	7.4%	8.9%	13.1%	10.0%
2 A-levels	15.6%	11.6%	18.1%	14.6%	15.0%
3 A-levels	5.1%	2.3%	4.3%	5.7%	4.2%
No answer	0.5%	1.0%	1.1%	0.7%	0.8%

Adults were much more ready to accept that formal qualifications were not required for mature entry to part-time degree courses: applicants, in particular, were fairly clear on the issue. The credit for this accurate perception might be largely due to the Open University, which emphasises in all its promotional material that formal qualifications are not required for entry to its degree programmes. This message is still not as widely understood, or accepted, as might have been hoped, however, since nearly half of all adults think that a solid set of school-leaving qualifications are necessary to study for a part-time degree. If higher education outside the Open University is serious about seeking to enrol adults lacking such qualifications, it will be important both to be clearer about the absence of formal requirements, and to ensure that admissions tutors do not in practice set barriers against those without such qualifications.

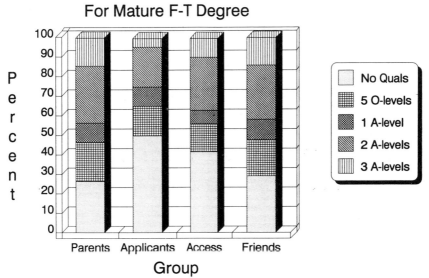

Chapter 6   Involvement in Higher Education

Two questions were included to check on adults' perceptions of the proportions of mature students in higher education. If higher education were considered by adults to be overwhelmingly populated by recent school-leavers, then it would not be surprising if they felt discomfort about the thought of returning to study. Higher education simply would not be geared up to their needs.

Question 11: *What percentage of* FULL-TIME *students in British higher education is mature (i.e. aged 25 or more)?*

Table 6.1: Adult Participation in Full-time Higher Education

Percentage	Parents	Applicants	Access	Friends	Total
5	14.3%	6.4%	5.5%	10.6%	9.1%
8	19.7%	13.5%	8.9%	14.2%	14.1%
11	23.7%	17.9%	13.5%	19.8%	18.6%
14	13.3%	15.4%	11.8%	13.0%	13.4%
17	8.8%	9.0%	12.8%	11.1%	10.4%
20	11.5%	14.9%	17.6%	15.2%	14.7%
23	3.4%	6.2%	6.9%	3.7%	5.2%
26	1.9%	5.5%	6.7%	4.4%	4.6%
29	1.0%	3.7%	3.2%	2.5%	2.6%
32	0.8%	3.1%	5.9%	3.1%	3.2%
35	0.4%	2.2%	3.3%	1.0%	1.8%
38	0.7%	1.4%	2.9%	1.2%	1.6%
No answer	0.4%	0.7%	0.9%	0.3%	0.6%
Average Answer	12.7%	16.4%	18.4%	15.1%	15.7%

The variation between the estimates of Parents and Access students is instructive. Parents, whose thoughts naturally focus on the 'traditional' applicants to higher education—their own offspring—gave a relatively low estimate of the number of mature students in higher education, at an average 12.7%. Access students, who by contrast will be focusing on the mature entrant to higher education, gave a very much higher estimate, at an average 18.4%. Applicants also gave a fairly high average estimate, of 16.4%.

These figures nevertheless refute the hypothesis that adults assume full-time higher education to be populated almost exclusively by recent school-leavers. All adult groups except Parents overestimated the number of students of 25 and over in higher education (the actual figure for 1988 was 14%[8]), and even Parents were not significantly adrift. There is certainly no need to mount any new information campaign which aims at showing adults that there are others like them in the higher education system.

Question 12: *What percentage of PART-TIME students in British higher education is mature (i.e. aged 25 or over)?*

Table 6.2: Adult Participation in Part-time Higher Education

Percentage	Parents	Applicants	Access	Friends	Total
5	4.3%	2.2%	1.5%	2.4%	2.6%
10	6.1%	5.1%	6.4%	7.7%	6.2%
15	13.7%	8.1%	8.9%	10.9%	10.4%
20	13.5%	9.6%	9.6%	12.7%	11.2%
25	11.6%	10.1%	12.3%	11.4%	11.3%
30	11.7%	10.7%	11.7%	11.9%	11.5%
35	8.3%	11.5%	12.7%	9.0%	10.5%
40	11.2%	11.3%	11.1%	10.8%	11.1%
45	3.9%	7.4%	6.2%	6.3%	5.9%
50	6.6%	7.3%	5.9%	6.9%	6.6%
55	3.4%	6.2%	6.0%	3.8%	5.0%
60	5.1%	9.6%	6.6%	5.7%	6.9%
No answer	0.4%	0.8%	0.9%	0.4%	0.6%
Average Answer	29.53%	34.49%	32.79%	30.96%	32.04%

The scattering of answers to this question was extremely wide, showing considerable uncertainty on the issue. The collective wisdom of adults might be taken to show a recognition that those aged 25 and over are well-represented in part-time higher education. Nevertheless, adults certainly did not realise just how very well represented mature students are in this mode of study. In fact 66% of part-time students in higher education, in 1988, were aged 25 or over.[9] Adults may not have

[8] *Education Statistics for the United Kingdom*, 1988 edition, page v.
[9] Ibid.

perceived part-time higher education as 'for' the under-twenty-f
neither did they realise the extent to which it is dominated by mature
students.

Once again, Parents gave lower estimates of the proportion of adults
taking part in higher education than Applicants and Access students, but
the margin was this time not wide.

Mature Student Success Rates

Anecdotal evidence from tutors of mature students would seem to
indicate that such students have significant doubts about their ability to
complete their studies successfully. It is frequently said that such
students require far more reassurance about their abilities than
traditional students. This would not be wholly surprising. Mature
students, after all, will often have been out of study for some
considerable period, and scholarly skills could thus be felt to be 'rusty'.

Question 13 was therefore set to test the hypothesis that potential mature
students were being kept away from higher education because of fears
about whether such students normally competed successfully with
younger students. If that were the case, then an information programme
which showed that mature students tend to cope very well with study—as
demonstrated by Bourner and Hamed[10]—would be of considerable
value.

The following findings, however, refute the hypothesis, and show once
again that such a campaign is unnecessary.

Question 13: *The standard of degree achieved by mature students, is, on*
average (tick one):

1 = significantly below that of traditional students
2 = somewhat below that of traditional students
3 = about the same as that of traditional students
4 = somewhat better than that of traditional students
5 = significantly better than that of traditional students

[10] *Entry Qualifications and Degree Performance* by Tom Bourner with Mahmoud
Hamed, CNAA Development Services Publication 10, 1987.

Table 6.3: Mature Student Success in Higher Education

	Parents	Applicants	Access	Friends	Total
1	1.6%	1.0%	0.9%	1.2%	1.2%
2	13.4%	4.6%	2.9%	11.1%	7.6%
3	24.5%	17.0%	16.3%	25.2%	20.3%
4	43.0%	48.9%	45.9%	43.4%	45.5%
5	17.0%	27.2%	32.1%	17.8%	24.1%
No answer	0.6%	1.4%	1.9%	1.3%	1.3%
Average	3.58	3.93	4.00	3.62	3.80

Adults seem, in fact, to be remarkably well aware of the relative success of mature students, with nearly three quarters getting the 'right' answer. Those particularly needing to know this—the Access students and Applicants—were in the least doubt, with 76.1% getting the 'right' answer. Much the most diffident were the Parents: 15% assumed that mature students performed less well than recent school-leavers, compared with only 3.8% of Access students.

Chapter 7   Recognition of Individual Institutions

Question 14: *Name three actual British institutions in each of the following categories: [universities, polytechnics, and colleges of higher education].*

This question was originally formulated with a view to checking the extent of the respondents' familiarity with polytechnics and colleges of higher education: the ability or inability to name such institutions would clearly be a useful indicator of the understanding of these sectors. It was assumed that respondents would have no difficulty at all in correctly naming three universities, and that any deviation from a 100% success rate would indicate misreading of the question or failure to complete the questionnaire. This assumption, though it would no doubt explain some of the deviation, nevertheless proved erroneous. A surprising number of cities were wrongly assumed to possess universities, and a remarkable number of institutions were wrongly assumed to be universities. Eton and Harrow might or might not be gratified to hear that they were each cited as universities on more than one occasion.

Table 7.1: Ability to Name Three Universities

	Parents	Applicants	Access	Friends	Total
Named 3	93.7%	89.3%	80.4%	88.3%	87.9%
Named 2	0.6%	2.0%	6.3%	2.9%	3.0%
Named 1	5.3%	7.4%	10.2%	6.2%	7.4%
Named 0	0.4%	1.3%	3.1%	2.5%	1.7%
Average number named	2.88 unis	2.79 unis	2.64 unis	2.77 unis	2.77 unis

Table 7.2: Ability to Name Three Polytechnics

	Parents	Applicants	Access	Friends	Total
Named 3	79.7%	75.8%	45.0%	66.2%	66.7%
Named 2	12.1%	10.5%	24.0%	17.5%	15.9%
Named 1	7.1%	10.9%	22.1%	11.6%	13.1%
Named 0	1.0%	2.8%	8.8%	4.6%	4.3%
Average number named	2.71 polys	2.59 polys	2.05 polys	2.45 polys	2.45 polys

Table 7.3: Ability to Name Three Colleges of Higher Education

	Parents	Applicants	Access	Friends	Total
Named 3	19.0%	16.4%	5.1%	13.1%	13.4%
Named 2	20.8%	17.1%	8.9%	16.4%	15.7%
Named 1	27.3%	30.3%	27.5%	31.0%	28.8%
Named 0	32.9%	36.3%	59.4%	39.5%	42.0%

Average
number named   1.26 CHEs 1.13 CHEs 0.61 CHEs 1.03 CHEs 1.00 CHEs

The Parents' ability to name three universities was virtually identical to the average ability, at 93.9%, of sixth-formers. However, Parents proved much more able to name three polytechnics than were lower-sixth-formers (53.8%), but somewhat less able than upper-sixth-formers (86.8%). They were also far more able to name colleges of higher education than either lower-sixth-formers (5.1%) or upper-sixth-formers (15.3%).

This relative success was very definitely not duplicated by Access students, who were by far the weakest group of the adults on this question, and weaker than sixth-formers on all three elements. It is perhaps surprising that almost one in five of this group did not successfully answer the question 'name three universities', and the group's abilities to name polytechnics and CHEs was very markedly below that of the other adult groups. Again, the very high degree of ignorance amongst Access students of the colleges of higher education must be a cause for concern, in light of the particular relevance of these institutions to Access students.

The results from Friends were surprisingly close to those of Applicants, given the obvious need of the latter to understand what higher education has to offer. It is interesting that a quarter of the Applicants could not name three polytechnics. This would seem to be due to adult Applicants focusing their interests, unlike sixth-formers, on a small number of institutions.

Recognition of Individual Institutions

Each respondent was asked to name three universities, three polytechnics, and three colleges of higher education, and as a result some

21,000 'namings' were recorded. The frequency of mention of each institution is indicated in the following three tables.

As shown in *Young People's Knowledge*, there is a general correlation between relative mention-frequency and relative attractiveness, and thus the tables below give some clue to the relative competitiveness of each institution. 'Reminder' (prompted recall) tests, of course, can give results significantly at variance from 'recall' tests. Nevertheless, the low positions given to important London institutions such as LSE[11], Imperial College, and UCL should not be seen as making the tables meaningless. Those working in higher education may indeed perceive these institutions as prestigious; it does not follow that the general public does so.

The league tables are, in general, remarkably similar to those provided by sixth-formers, and give further verification to the principles recorded in *Young People's Knowledge*, which are that:

1. Institutions named after well-known and distinctive towns and cities significantly outperform those named after lesser-known towns and cities.

2. Institutions named after town or cities, even the lesser-known ones, significantly outperform those named after regions.

3. Institutions named after places, be they towns or regions, significantly outperform those named after people, concepts, or rivers.

Notes

1. All percentages represent the proportion of respondents that included the institution as one of their three choices for the sector.

2. Figures in brackets represent the 'league table' position.

3. The table positions correctly give the order of precedence of each HEI, though this is not in all instances apparent from the percentages which, for simplicity, are given to just one decimal place.

---

[11] Note that a separate Heist 'reminder' survey of 1,000 lower-sixth-formers showed that they had a lower opinion of the London School of Economics than Stockton University (which of course does not exist).

4. The 'Total' column is calculated on an unweighted-average basis: i.e. no attempt has been made to compensate for the relative under-representation of the 'Friends' category.

5. Wide allowance was made for name changes and for 'near misses'. 'Lanchester', for instance, was accepted as 'Coventry Polytechnic', and 'Pontypridd Polytechnic' as 'Polytechnic of Wales'.

Table 7.4: Universities Named

University	Parents	Applicants	Access	Friends	Total
Aberdeen	0.9% (42)	1.1% (40)	1.0% (41)	1.6% (36)	1.1% (41)
Aberystwyth	0.9% (43)	0.9% (43)	2.1% (32)	1.5% (38)	1.3% (39)
Aston	4.5% (18)	3.4% (27)	3.9% (20)	4.3% (20)	4.0% (22)
Bangor	1.4% (38)	1.6% (38)	1.8% (37)	1.2% (42)	1.6% (38)
Bath	3.9% (22)	5.5% (15)	3.7% (21)	3.5% (22)	4.2% (20)
Belfast	0.3% (51)	0.5% (52)	1.2% (38)	1.0% (43)	0.7% (45)
Birmingham	12.7% (8)	7.7% (11)	7.0% (9)	10.5% (8)	9.4% (8)
Bradford	2.9% (27)	3.4% (27)	2.4% (29)	2.2% (30)	2.8% (29)
Bristol	17.0% (5)	14.1% (4)	10.4% (6)	11.9% (6)	13.5% (5)
Buckingham	0.2% (53)	0.2% (56)	0.0% (58=)	0.0% (60)	0.1% (59)
Brunel	1.1% (39)	1.7% (37)	2.6% (26)	1.6% (34)	1.8% (36)
Cambridge	27.3% (2)	26.1% (2)	38.8% (2)	33.2% (2)	31.2% (2)
Cardiff	4.2% (20)	5.4% (17)	5.1% (17)	5.0% (19)	4.9% (16)
City	0.3% (50)	0.8% (46)	0.5% (48)	0.6% (46)	0.5% (49)
Dundee	1.0% (40)	0.5% (51)	0.2% (53)	0.3% (53)	0.5% (50)
Durham	14.2% (6)	11.5% (6)	10.7% (4)	10.9% (7)	11.9% (6)
East Anglia	2.7% (28)	2.5% (33)	2.0% (34)	2.8% (25)	2.5% (31)
Edinburgh	4.4% (19)	4.5% (22)	5.9% (13)	4.0% (21)	4.8% (17)
Essex	2.0% (34)	1.8% (35)	1.9% (35)	1.8% (33)	1.9% (35)
Exeter	7.3% (12)	7.9% (9)	7.5% (8)	6.0% (15)	7.3% (11)
Glasgow	1.5% (36)	1.7% (36)	2.9% (25)	1.8% (32)	2.0% (34)
Heriot-Watt	0.5% (46)	0.4% (53)	0.7% (44)	0.4% (51)	0.5% (48)
Hull	4.9% (15)	5.1% (18)	5.5% (14)	6.3% (13)	5.4% (14)
Keele	3.6% (25)	6.3% (14)	2.4% (30)	6.2% (14)	4.5% (18)
Kent	1.9% (35)	2.8% (32)	5.5% (15)	6.5% (12)	3.9% (23)
Lampeter	0.2% (52)	0.5% (50)	0.0% (58=)	0.9% (44)	0.4% (53)
Lancaster	3.8% (23)	4.3% (23)	3.5% (22)	3.4% (23)	3.8% (24)
Leeds	17.4% (3)	13.5% (5)	11.9% (3)	14.0% (5)	14.2% (4)

Table 7.4: Universities Named—*continued*

University	Parents	Applicants	Access	Friends	Total
Leicester	3.4% (26)	4.0% (24)	2.5% (27)	1.6% (35)	3.0% (27)
Liverpool	12.9% (7)	7.9% (10)	6.1% (11)	14.3% (4)	9.9% (7)
London	9.8% (9)	9.7% (7)	9.3% (7)	6.0% (16)	9.0% (9)
Goldsmiths'	0.1% (57)	0.5% (49)	0.2% (52)	0.0% (57=)	0.2% (54)
Imperial C	0.2% (56)	0.4% (54)	0.1% (56)	0.1% (55)	0.2% (55)
King's C	0.7% (45)	0.8% (45)	0.6% (46)	0.3% (54)	0.7% (46)
LSE	0.5% (47)	0.8% (47)	0.9% (43)	0.0% (57=)	0.6% (47)
Q. Mary	0.1% (59)	0.2% (59)	0.1% (54)	0.4% (49)	0.2% (56)
UCL	0.1% (58)	0.9% (44)	0.9% (42)	1.3% (40)	0.8% (44)
Hol & Bed	0.2% (55)	0.3% (55)	0.1% (57)	0.0% (57=)	0.2% (57)
Wye	0.0% (60)	0.0% (60)	0.0% (58=)	0.3% (52)	0.1% (60)
Loughb'ro	2.2% (32)	3.0% (31)	2.1% (33)	2.9% (24)	2.5% (30)
Manchester	17.1% (4)	15.7% (3)	10.5% (5)	16.8% (3)	14.8% (3)
UMIST	0.9% (44)	1.9% (34)	0.6% (47)	1.5% (39)	1.2% (40)
Newcastle	6.9% (13)	7.6% (13)	6.1% (12)	8.0% (9)	7.0% (13)
Nottingham	8.8% (11)	8.2% (8)	4.3% (19)	7.2% (11)	7.1% (11)
Open	0.2% (54)	0.2% (57)	0.1% (55)	0.1% (56)	0.2% (55)
Oxford	35.4% (1)	36.5% (1)	44.8% (1)	36.9% (1)	38.6% (1)
Reading	4.6% (17)	4.6% (21)	3.0% (24)	2.4% (29)	3.8% (25)
St Andrews	2.1% (33)	1.3% (39)	1.1% (40)	1.9% (31)	1.6% (37)
Salford	2.7% (29)	3.0% (30)	1.1% (39)	1.5% (37)	2.1% (33)
Sheffield	9.3% (10)	7.7% (12)	6.3% (10)	7.5% (10)	7.7% (10)
South'ton	3.9% (21)	3.8% (25)	3.1% (23)	2.5% (26)	3.4% (26)
Stirling	1.0% (41)	0.9% (41)	0.6% (45)	1.2% (41)	0.9% (42)
Strathclyde	0.4% (48)	0.9% (42)	0.3% (51)	0.4% (49)	0.5% (51)
Surrey	2.5% (31)	3.3% (28)	1.9% (36)	0.7% (45)	2.3% (32)
Sussex	2.6% (30)	5.5% (16)	4.9% (18)	2.5% (27)	4.0% (21)
Swansea	3.7% (24)	3.1% (29)	2.5% (28)	2.5% (28)	3.0% (28)
Ulster	0.4% (49)	0.2% (58)	0.5% (50)	0.4% (52)	0.4% (52)
Wales	1.5% (37)	0.6% (48)	0.3% (50)	0.6% (47)	0.8% (43)
Warwick	5.2% (14)	4.6% (20)	2.3% (31)	5.5% (18)	4.3% (19)
York	4.9% (16)	5.1% (19)	5.4% (16)	5.5% (17)	5.2% (15)

Examination of the above table shows that certain universities were relatively favoured or disfavoured by each group of adults. In some cases a pattern is apparent; in others the authors were not able to discern a specific pattern.

Parents were disproportionately aware of the more prestigious, longer-established universities, and gave notably higher scores for Birmingham, Bristol, Durham, Leeds, and Sheffield. This is perhaps to be explained by a parental preference to see offspring placed in institutions felt to be in an 'ivy league'. Parents were disproportionately less likely to mention Brunel and Kent.

Access students proved significantly more likely to mention Oxford and Cambridge than the other adult groups. This would seem to indicate a relatively lower awareness of the breadth of the university sector. Pupils at the beginning of their lower-sixth year showed a similar disproportionate tendency to mention Oxford and Cambridge; as their knowledge of the sector increased, so awareness of other universities pushed Oxbridge further from the forefront of their consciousness.

Access students were significantly *less* likely than other adult groups to mention Birmingham, Bristol, Durham, East Anglia, Keele, Liverpool, Manchester, Nottingham, and Warwick—a list which significantly includes those prestigious universities that particularly commended themselves to parents.

Applicants were disproportionately likely to mention Bath, Bradford, Keele, Leicester, Surrey and Sussex, and disproportionately less likely than other adult groups to mention Aston.

Friends were disproportionately likely to mention Kent, Hull, and Liverpool, and disproportionately less likely to mention Exeter, Leicester, London, Reading, Southampton, Surrey and Sussex.

It is perhaps surprising that the Open University, which was created specifically with the needs of adults in mind, and achieves a high profile through media coverage, nevertheless received so few mentions. It is also interesting that the 'private' universities, Buckingham and Cranfield, are almost completely unrecognised. Only one adult in a thousand mentioned Buckingham, while none mentioned Cranfield.

Comparisons with sixth-formers indicate that adults are much more aware of Cardiff, Keele and Sussex. A likely explanation is that parents are more sensitive than sixth-formers to institutions that have been named in the media.

Table 7.5: Polytechnics Named

Polytechnic	Parents	Applicants	Access	Friends	Total
Birmingham	9.8% (12)	8.4% (13)	10.8% (3)	11.2% (8)	10.1% (10)
Bournemouth	1.6% (29)	1.5% (31)	1.8% (31)	0.9% (32)	1.5% (32)
Brighton	6.2% (19)	9.3% (11)	5.7% (17)	8.9% (11)	7.5% (12)
Bristol	14.9% (7)	13.3% (5)	9.8% (4)	11.6% (7)	12.4% (8)
City	1.1% (30)	4.0% (29)	2.8% (28)	2.1% (29)	2.5% (29)
Coventry	8.4% (14)	6.1% (21)	3.2% (27)	5.1% (20)	5.7% (21)
East London	0.9% (32)	3.8% (30)	3.3% (26)	1.6% (31)	2.4% (31)
Hatfield	7.8% (15)	4.5% (26)	5.9% (16)	6.3% (18)	6.0% (16)
Huddersfield	7.2% (16)	7.0% (19)	3.5% (25)	3.7% (24)	5.4% (22)
Humberside	2.9% (25)	1.3% (32)	3.7% (24)	1.9% (30)	2.4% (30)
Kingston	10.4% (11)	6.7% (20)	4.4% (20)	6.7% (17)	7.0% (15)
Lancashire	7.0% (17)	4.3% (27)	5.1% (19)	6.7% (16)	5.8% (19)
Leeds	14.2% (8)	12.9% (6)	11.9% (2)	15.0% (4)	13.5% (4)
Leicester	8.9% (13)	8.0% (14)	4.2% (21)	7.1% (14)	7.1% (14)
Liverpool	16.4% (6)	11.5% (9)	9.5% (6)	18.8% (2)	14.0% (2)
Manchester	22.6% (1)	19.6% (1)	13.6% (1)	20.5% (1)	19.1% (1)
Middlesex	4.4% (22)	7.4% (16)	7.9% (14)	4.6% (21)	6.1% (18)
Newcastle	12.6% (9)	12.5% (7)	8.4% (10)	10.9% (9)	11.1% (9)
Nottingham	19.0% (2)	13.6% (4)	6.9% (15)	16.7% (3)	14.0% (3)
Oxford	17.0% (4)	13.7% (3)	9.2% (8)	10.3% (10)	12.5% (6)
PCL	1.0% (31)	7.0% (17)	4.2% (22)	2.7% (28)	3.7% (26)
PNL	2.4% (28)	7.9% (15)	8.6% (9)	4.0% (22)	5.7% (20)
Portsmouth	16.4% (5)	11.5% (8)	9.7% (5)	12.2% (6)	12.4% (7)
Sheffield	17.4% (3)	14.1% (2)	8.0% (12)	13.8% (5)	13.4% (5)
South Bank	2.7% (26)	7.0% (18)	3.9% (23)	3.4% (25)	4.2% (24)
South West	10.6% (10)	9.5% (10)	9.5% (7)	8.8% (12)	9.6% (11)
Staffordshire	6.0% (20)	5.0% (22)	1.5% (32)	7.4% (13)	5.0% (23)
Sunderland	6.6% (18)	9.1% (12)	8.4% (11)	5.5% (19)	7.4% (13)
Teesside	3.3% (23)	4.6% (25)	5.3% (18)	3.3% (26)	4.1% (25)
Thames	2.6% (27)	4.8% (24)	2.2% (30)	4.0% (23)	3.4% (27)
Wales	3.2% (24)	4.0% (28)	2.7% (29)	1.2% (27)	3.2% (28)
Wolv'hpton	4.7% (21)	4.9% (23)	8.0% (13)	6.7% (15)	6.1% (17)

Adults were far more conscious than sixth formers of PNL, and significantly more conscious of PCL, South Bank, Staffordshire, Teesside, Thames, and Wales. They were less conscious than sixth-formers of: Coventry, Hatfield, Huddersfield, Newcastle, Oxford, and Polytechnic South West.

Not surprisingly, parents were much less likely than other adult groups to be aware of PNL, City, East London, PCL, Middlesex, and South Bank—the polytechnics that have a high mature student intake. Parents were distinctly more aware than other adult groups of Bristol, Hatfield, Huddersfield, Kingston, Nottingham, Oxford, Portsmouth and Sheffield.

Applicants were more likely than average to refer to Brighton, City, East London, PCL, South Bank, and Thames, and less likely to refer to Birmingham, Hatfield, Humberside, and Lancashire.

Access students were dramatically less likely than other adult groups to refer to Nottingham, Sheffield, and Staffordshire, and were somewhat less likely than average to refer to Brighton, Coventry, Kingston, Leicester, Liverpool, and Thames. They were dramatically more likely than other adult groups to refer to PNL, and somewhat more likely to refer to East London, Humberside, PCL, and Wolverhampton.

The awareness of Friends did not prove widely at variance with other groups, and could almost serve as a 'control' group to this question, since they gave each institution a number of mentions close to the overall average.

Colleges of Higher Education

The following table of CHEs is not divided into the usual four groups, since the low total numbers of mentions could lead to misleading comparisons. The safest comparisons would be between adults as a whole and sixth-formers as a whole. On this basis, the following institutions seem to have higher awareness levels amongst adults: Derbyshire and St Mark & St John, by a substantial margin, and Crewe & Alsager, Ealing, West Sussex, West London, and West Glamorgan, by a lesser margin.

The following institutions were disproportionately disfavoured by adults: Charlotte Mason, by a substantial margin, and Nene, Norwich, and Ripon & York, by a lesser margin.

Table 7.6: CHEs Named

HE	Total	CHE	Total
Anglia CHE	4.4% (3)	Loughborough CA	0.6% (45)
Bangor Normal Coll	0.6% (45)	Luton CHE	2.7% (16)
Bath CHE	4.4% (2)	St Mark & St John	2.1% (21)
Bedford CHE	2.7% (17)	Nene Coll	3.0% (12)
Bishop Grosseteste	0.5% (46)	NEWI	0.5% (49)
Bolton IHE	3.8% (5)	New College Durham	1.7% (26)
Bradford/Ilkley Col	2.0% (23)	Newman & Westfield	0.2% (55)
Bretton Hall College	1.5% (29)	North Riding Coll	0.6% (44)
Buckingham CHE	1.9% (25)	North Cheshire Coll	0.7% (41)
Bulmershe College	0.9% (36)	Norwich City Coll	0.9% (34)
Camborne S of Mines	0.3% (53)	Ripon & York St John	2.1% (22)
Canterbury CC Coll	2.8% (15)	Roehampton HE	2.2% (20)
Charlotte Mason HE	0.6% (43)	Rolle College	0.5% (48)
Cheltenham & Gloucs	3.2% (10)	Royal Coll of Music	0.1% (60)
Crewe and Alsager	3.9% (4)	Salford Coll of Tech	1.2% (31)
Dartington College	0.4% (52)	South Glamorgan HE	2.2% (18)
Derbyshire CHE	5.1% (1)	Southampton Institute	2.2% (19)
Doncaster Coll	0.9% (35)	S Martin's Coll	1.0% (33)
[12]Dorset Institute	3.7% (7)	St Mary's Twickenham	0.8% (39)
Ealing CHE	3.0% (13)	SW London Coll	0.1% (56)
Edge Hill CHE	3.5% (9)	Thames Valley Coll	0.4% (50)
Falmouth Sch Art	0.1% (58)	Trinity Carmarthen	0.2% (54)
Gwent CHE	0.8% (38)	Trinity & All Saints	1.6% (28)
Harper Adams	0.1% (59)	West Sussex HE	1.9% (24)
Homerton Coll	0.1% (57)	West London HE	1.3% (30)
[12]Humberside CHE	3.2% (11)	West Glamorgan HE	1.7% (27)
King Alfred's Coll	1.1% (32)	Westminster, Oxford	0.7% (40)
La Sainte Union CHE	0.7% (42)	Winchester Coll of Art	0.8% (37)
Liverpool Institute	2.9% (14)	Worcester HE	3.8% (6)
London Institute	0.4% (51)		

---

[12] Dorset and Humberside were accepted in both the "polytechnic" and "CHE" categories, since they were in transition during the survey period.

Ability to Name Three HEIs

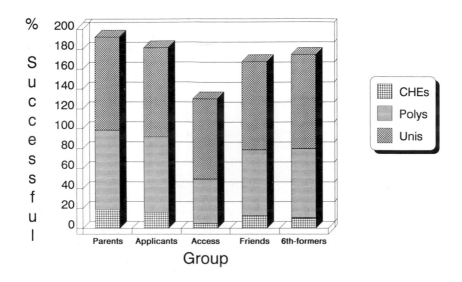

Chapter 8   Sources of Knowledge about Higher Education

Question 15: *List your sources of knowledge about higher education, in order of priority. If none, say 'None'.*

The following table indicates the proportion of adults in each group mentioning a particular information source.

Table 8.1: Sources of Information

	Parents	Applicants	Access	Friends	Total
'None'	36.9% (1)	23.1% (4)	39.3% (1)	41.6% (1)	34.5% (1)
Careers[13]	7.9% (9)	30.0% (1)	16.0% (3)	19.8% (2)	18.3% (2)
Prospectuses	11.1% (7)	27.4% (2)	16.0% (2)	13.3% (3)	17.3% (3)
PCAS	13.0% (5)	26.8% (3)	5.0% (9)	8.8% (6)	13.9% (4)
Newspapers	20.3% (2)	9.7% (8)	9.2% (6)	13.1% (4)	13.0% (5)
Library	7.0% (10)	17.0% (6)	15.6% (4)	8.3% (8)	12.4% (6)
UCCA	13.8% (4)	18.4% (5)	5.1% (8)	8.5% (7)	11.8% (7)
FE Colleges	3.0% (13)	9.3% (7)	8.5% (5)	3.1% (12)	6.3% (8)
Schools	12.7% (6)	4.6% (13)	3.4% (12)	10.9% (5)	7.6% (9)
Guides	9.6% (8)	8.3% (9)	2.2% (15)	4.9% (11)	6.4% (10)
Children	18.0% (3)	0.2% (30)	1.1% (18)	3.2% (15)	5.9% (11)
Friends	2.3% (14)	7.9% (10)	6.0% (7)	6.5% (9)	5.6% (12)
Books	5.0% (11)	5.1% (11)	4.0% (11)	3.7% (14)	4.5% (13)
HEIs	4.1% (12)	4.9% (12)	2.9% (13)	5.5% (10)	4.2% (14)
Grapevine	1.6% (16)	3.0% (14)	4.0% (10)	1.3% (19)	2.6% (15)
Family	1.4% (18)	1.7% (15)	2.0% (16)	4.3% (13)	2.1% (16)
Leaflets	1.0% (19)	1.7% (16)	2.3% (14)	1.9% (16)	1.7% (17)
Students	0.6% (23)	1.2% (19)	1.0% (19)	1.6% (18)	1.0% (18)
TV	1.4% (17)	0.4% (24)	0.6% (22)	1.9% (17)	1.0% (19)
HE experience	2.3% (15)	0.1% (34)	0.3% (29)	1.3% (20)	1.0% (20)
Media	0.6% (24)	0.9% (20)	0.7% (21)	0.9% (21)	0.8% (21)
Prof bodies	0.7% (22)	1.4% (18)	0.3% (31)	0.3% (30)	0.7% (22)
Adult ed	0.1% (34)	0.8% (21)	1.6% (17)	0.0% (35)	0.7% (23)
LEA	0.4% (27)	1.6% (17)	0.1% (35)	0.4% (29)	0.6% (24)
Adverts	0.8% (21)	0.6% (22)	0.4% (26)	0.4% (28)	0.6% (25)

[13] This includes 'careers library', 'careers office', 'careers adviser', and just 'careers'.

	Parents	Applicants	Access	Friends	Total
Radio	0.6% (25)	0.3% (28)	0.6% (23)	0.9% (22)	0.6% (26)
Work colleagues	0.8% (20)	0.3% (29)	0.3% (28)	0.6% (26)	0.5% (27)
Magazines	0.2% (32)	0.5% (23)	0.4% (27)	0.7% (23)	0.4% (28)
Job centres	0.2% (31)	0.2% (32)	0.7% (20)	0.6% (25)	0.4% (29)
Open Uni	0.3% (28)	0.4% (25)	0.3% (30)	0.4% (27)	0.3% (30)
Careers conventions	0.4% (26)	0.4% (26)	0.2% (33)	0.1% (33)	0.3% (31)
Open days	0.2% (30)	0.4% (27)	0.5% (25)	0.1% (32)	0.3% (32)
Visits	0.2% (33)	0.2% (31)	0.3% (32)	0.7% (24)	0.3% (33)
Videos	0.0% (35)	0.1% (35)	0.5% (24)	0.0% (34)	0.2% (34)
Posters	0.3% (29)	0.1% (33)	0.1% (34)	0.2% (31)	0.1% (35)

Much the most popular response overall to the question, given by more than a third of respondents, was *None*. Perhaps it is not surprising that so many Friends should provide such an answer, since this group could not be expected to be looking actively for information about higher education. It is worrying, though, that almost a quarter of adult Applicants felt that they had no sources of information worth mentioning. It is distinctly alarming that almost 40% of Access students should say likewise. They are on courses which are designed to prepare them for higher education, and it is difficult to see how this could be successful if no access to information about higher education is provided.[14]

Adults who did refer to sources of information gave a very diverse range of sources: this was particularly the case for Applicants, who gave an average of 2.63 sources, compared to 2.01 by Parents, 1.87 by Friends, and just 1.67 by Access students. Some information sources that might have been expected to be influential, nevertheless turned out to receive very few mentions: all things being equal, this would indicate that they have extremely limited influence. Videos, magazines and careers conventions would seem to have as little influence on adults' views of higher education as they do on sixth-formers[15]. Open days, which had some noticeable effect on sixth-formers (7.4%), received very few mentions from adults. As in most surveys about higher education, advertisements received a very low rating; even Parents, who might have been thought fairly sensitive to advertisements about higher education, made very little reference to them. Also mentioned by just 0.6% of adults was *Radio*, a medium which often receives significant amounts of attention from higher education public relations and marketing personnel.

[14] In fairness to Access courses it must, however, be pointed out that the students would have been at an early stage of the Access programme, and thus would have had relatively little opportunity to benefit from any information made available through the course.

[15] Videos were mentioned by 1.7% of sixth-formers, and careers conventions by 1.2%. Magazines received too few mentions to be identified separately.

The Open University received surprisingly few mentions in view of its accessibility through TV and radio broadcasts. It is possible, however, that the OU is considered to be *sui generis*, separate from the rest of higher education, rather than part and parcel of it. The very low numbers of mentions of the OU given in answers to Question 14 tend to reinforce this interpretation.

Newspapers proved to be much more influential amongst adults—particularly Parents—than amongst sixth-formers (3.8%). This conclusion is reinforced by the responses to Question 14, which indicated that adults are much more sensitive than sixth-formers to institutions 'in the news'. Nevertheless, the two groups that higher education would wish to address directly through the newspapers—Access students and adult Applicants—were the least likely to refer to newspapers as a source. Interestingly, Parents were twice as likely to mention newspapers as any other adult group. For readers wondering which newspapers were mentioned by name[16] most often, the figures are: *The Times* (57 mentions), *The Guardian* (53), *The Sunday Times* (17), *The Observer* (12), *The Times Educational Supplement* (12), *The Times Higher Educational Supplement* (11), *The Daily Telegraph* (9), various special supplements (8), and *The Independent* (6). Not surprisingly, no adult owned up to having read anything other than a 'quality' newspaper.

The single source of information most frequently referred to was 'prospectuses' (see below for 'careers'), mentioned by 693 respondents. Editors of prospectuses might be gratified by yet another indication of the widespread influence of this publication. Nevertheless, only 16% of Access students, and 27.4% of adult Applicants, referred to prospectuses: a much lower figure than that given by sixth-formers (47.6% overall, and 64.9% at the start of the upper-sixth). Much more determined attempts to ensure that course information is made available to these two groups might thus be called for. HEIs would be advised to ensure that Access courses in their region were well supplied with stocks of literature promoting courses.

Though prospectuses were the most frequently mentioned single influence, 95 adults listed 'careers library', 192 'careers office', 95 'careers advisers', and 419 'careers' without any further modification. 731 individuals, therefore, referred to 'careers' in some shape or form,

---

[16] Most—336 respondents—referred just to 'newspapers' *per se*, rather than to any specific newspaper.

making the combined category the most popular amongst adults.[17] Applicants showed a particularly high propensity to refer to this influence: a point that should be carefully noted by higher education information officers. It would seem that the majority of respondents were referring to careers offices outside schools and colleges—outlets which can sometimes receive relatively little attention from higher education.

Naturally enough, adults and sixth-formers gave very different emphasis to certain influences. 18% of Parents gave 'children' as a source, which we would hardly expect to see repeated by sixth-formers[18]. Students, again, were understandably a lot more influential amongst sixth-formers (10.2%) than amongst adults. Similarly, while teachers were highly influential amongst sixth-formers (34.3%), they received few mentions from adults. In the above table, 'school teachers' were subsumed within 'school', and 'college tutors' within 'FE college'. If disaggregated, however, the latter two categories would gain the following percentages of mentions:

Table 8.2: References to Teachers & Tutors

	Parents	Applicants	Access	Friends	Total
School teachers	0.54%	1.36%	0.36%	1.47%	0.88%
College tutors	0.45%	2.89%	4.34%	0.88%	2.88%

As can be seen, even Access students—the only adults in the group that can be assumed to have current access to teachers or tutors—gave few mentions of teachers/tutors.

'Guides' and 'books', which were quite influential amongst sixth-formers, retained at least some of their influence amongst adults. Parents and Applicants made fairly frequent references to guides, either generically, or by name. Access students made markedly fewer references to guides—far fewer even than Friends, which might seem odd, in view of their strong implicit interest in, and need to know about, higher education. It is arguable that such guides should be made as readily available to Access students as they are in well-organised sixth-forms.

[17] A small number of respondents (27) entered 'schools careers office', and such answers were thus classified under 'schools'. It is likely that the majority of other references to 'careers' referred to careers services outside schools and colleges, but this cannot be certain.

[18] It is perhaps odd that extremely few Applicants referred to children, since the age range of this group is known to be wide—much wider, indeed, than amongst the Friends, who were 32 times more likely to mention children. This oddity could well be worthy of further exploration.

Those guides mentioned specifically by name included: *Brian Heap's guides/Degree Course Offers, NatWest Guide, Which Degree Course, Students' Guide to Universities, Polytechnics and CHEs, CRAC Directory, Mature Students' Handbook, Readers' Digest Careers Guide, Degree Directory*, and *The Potter University Guides*.

PCAS and UCCA guides were subsumed under the titles 'PCAS' and 'UCCA', both of which were mentioned more often by adults than by sixth-formers. It is curious that Access students should mention PCAS and UCCA much less often than other adult groups. The situation closely mirrors that with respect to Guides: it remains distinctly odd that Access students should be so averse to these standard sources of information about higher education. Access students, did, however, join Applicants in an increased propensity to refer to the library.

The category 'books' is inevitably vague, and those referring to this source may in some cases have been thinking of prospectuses or guides. However, some referred to books by name, and these included: *The Student Book, A Career in Law, Careers in Sport and Recreation, It is Never Too Late, Staying the Course*, and *The Yellow Pages*.

A point of sociological interest is that the 85 references to 'family' (parent, husband, wife, brother, sister) showed a curious male bias. Seven respondents gave 'husband' as a source, but none gave 'wife'; eleven referred to 'brother', but four to 'sister'. This imbalance could only be partially explained by the predominance of females in the survey.

Chapter 9   Possible Involvement in Higher Education

Qualifications Gained by Respondents

Question 16: *What is your highest level of academic qualifications achieved (tick one)*

1. *No formal qualifications*
2. *O-levels or equivalent*
3. *A-levels or equivalent*
4. *Higher National Diploma or equivalent*
5. *Degree*

Table 9.1: Highest Qualifications Obtained

	Parents	Applicants	Access	Friends	Total
1. No formal	11.8%	4.2%	20.1%	8.8%	9.4%
2. O-levels	28.1%	20.1%	56.7%	28.6%	31.7%
3. A-levels	17.0%	65.8%	17.2%	36.4%	47.3%
4. HND	15.0%	6.4%	3.1%	9.0%	5.9%
5. Degree	28.0%	3.2%	1.7%	16.3%	5.0%
6. No answer	0.2%	0.3%	1.1%	0.9%	0.6%

As can be seen, Parents had substantially the highest level of educational qualification, with 43% qualified to the HND or degree level—a level far in excess of the general population. This gives strong support to the findings from various sources that parental possession of a higher education qualification is one of the most powerful indicators of propensity to enter HE. (See also **Table 10.3.**)

As would be expected, few Applicants possessed degrees or their equivalent: what is much more surprising is that approximately two-thirds considered themselves to possess A-levels or their equivalent. It tends to be assumed that the 'older mature' applicant does not in general possess qualifications of this level, and thus requires dispensation from the usual requirements. The fact that such a high proportion of adult applicants *does* possess such qualifications again suggests that those lacking formal qualifications do not consider themselves suitable or acceptable to higher education, and are much less likely to come forward.

Friends were on average educated to a significantly higher level than the general population in the 25–35 age range. This again is unsurprising: the intention had been to focus on a group which, by its association with a degree applicant, was more likely than average to have an interest in higher education.

Access students possessed by far the lowest level of formal qualification, with more than three-quarters being educated to O-level standard at highest. This would partly explain the limited performance of this group on the various 'right or wrong' questions in this survey.

Highest Qualifications Obtained

Interest in Study at a University or Polytechnic

Question 17: *On a scale of 1 to 5, are you at all likely to apply for a course in a university? (Circle one number: 1 = not at all likely; 5 = extremely likely)*

Table 9.2: Interest in University Study

	Parents	Applicants	Access	Friends	Total
1	72.2%	32.0%	24.1%	42.9%	42.8%
2	10.4%	11.6%	13.7%	13.3%	12.1%
3	7.3%	15.3%	20.8%	13.6%	14.3%
4	2.1%	7.9%	12.2%	5.6%	7.1%
5	9.0%	33.2%	29.2%	24.6%	23.7%
Average Answer	1.63	2.99	3.09	2.56	2.57

Question 18: *On a scale of 1 to 5, are you at all likely to apply for a course in a polytechnic? (Circle one number: 1 = not at all likely; 5 = extremely likely)*

Table 9.3: Interest in Polytechnic Study

	Parents	Applicants	Access	Friends	Total
1	71.0%	8.4%	11.7%	40.0%	32.0%
2	11.5%	3.3%	7.6%	10.9%	8.1%
3	8.7%	11.0%	19.8%	14.9%	13.5%
4	3.3%	12.6%	17.4%	9.1%	10.8%
5	5.3%	64.6%	43.4%	25.1%	35.6%
Average Answer	1.60	4.22	3.73	2.68	3.10

It is noticeable that Parents expressed by far the least interest of the four groups in applying to study at a university, and even less interest in studying at a polytechnic. This would be partly explicable by the fact that a substantial proportion already possess higher education qualifications, combined with the greater average age of this group. It remains disappointing, nevertheless, that Parents so clearly perceive education as something that *stops* at a certain age. Almost three-quarters of a group which is closely involved in higher education does not perceive it as relevant to themselves at their stage of life. Studies in North America, where continuous professional development is a much more accepted part of the culture, show far higher levels of interest from adult groups.[19]

Parents were alone in indicating a greater interest in applying for courses in universities than in polytechnics. The other three groups demonstrated considerably higher interest in polytechnic courses. This is perhaps unsurprising, given the greater commitment of polytechnics to the non-traditional student, but the polytechnics will be gratified that their message has been getting across. Those interested in the continued widening of access might justifiably seek to ensure that the abandonment of the title 'polytechnic' does not prove to be a retrograde step.

At first there seems to be something odd about the Applicants' responses. They participated in the survey because they were applicants

[19] A study for the University of Northern British Columbia showed that 49% of the local adult population said they were 'very likely' to apply for a course at the University.

to *both* UCCA and PCAS, and yet they show a distinct lack of interest in one sector or the other. This may be because the survey was conducted shortly before the beginning of the academic year, by which time many applicants may have been accepted or rejected by a particular university, polytechnic or college as appropriate.

The figures for Access students shed considerable light on the commitment of such students to higher education. There is substantial anecdotal evidence that many such students are not taking their course with a view to entering college, polytechnic, or university. For instance, a Heist researcher, on questioning a group of Access students, was surprised to find that many did not even realise that successful completion of their course would furnish them with entry qualifications to higher education.[20] The students explained that they were studying for the sake of the course itself, and not because of any intentions to gain further qualifications; the role of the course in facilitating entrance to higher education had never been explained to them.

Further analysis of the questionnaires showed that just 14.1% of Access students said that they were 'extremely likely' to apply to both polytechnics and universities. 15.1% said they were extremely likely to apply to universities but not polytechnics, while 29.3% said they were extremely likely to apply to polytechnics but not universities. In all, 58.5% indicated that they were extremely likely to apply to a course in *either* a polytechnic or a university or both.

Further analysis also showed that 25.2% of the Access students entered neither '4' nor '5' to *either* question 17 or 18; a quarter of such students, therefore, expressed no particular interest in applying for a course in either universities or polytechnics. And as the table shows, 58.6% showed no particular interest in applying for a course in a university, while 39.1% showed no particular interest in applying for a course in a polytechnic. It is quite false, therefore, to treat all Access students as entrants-in-waiting to higher education. The Access course, clearly, serves a wider function.

One of the more encouraging aspects of the responses to questions 17 and 18 is that approximately one quarter of the Friends said that they were 'extremely likely' to apply for a course in a university, and a similar

---

[20] Note also the evidence of Table 5.1. 36.6% of Access course students said that the minimum entry requirements to a full-time degree course, for mature students, were two or three A-levels or their equivalent.

proportion said that they were extremely likely to apply to a course at a polytechnic. Since 12.4% said that they were extremely likely to apply for a course both at a university or a polytechnic, it follows that 37.3% said that they were extremely likely to apply for a course at *either* polytechnics or universities or both.

Confidence in Ability to Gain Information about HE

Question 19: *On a scale of 1 to 5, are you confident of being able to find information about courses of higher education if you need it?*

Table 9.4: Confidence in Ability to Find Information on HE

	Parents	Applicants	Access	Friends	Total
1	6.6%	3.1%	3.3%	4.9%	4.4%
2	5.2%	5.3%	6.9%	6.9%	6.0%
3	13.4%	15.9%	18.5%	17.5%	16.2%
4	16.9%	25.0%	25.6%	21.4%	22.3%
5	55.9%	50.7%	45.6%	49.3%	51.0%
Average	4.14	4.15	4.03	4.03	4.1

The answers to this question indicate that higher education is not perceived by the adults as being *difficult to get to know:* respondents indicated a remarkably high degree of confidence that they would be able to gain information about courses if they so chose. Almost three quarters rated their confidence as 'high' or 'very high', while only 10.4% demonstrated low confidence. Significantly, the group most likely to have been actively seeking information for themselves—the Applicants—showed the highest level of confidence that they could find the information they needed, so there is no evidence of confidence proving to be misplaced when put to the test.

The limited understanding of higher education demonstrated by adults earlier in this report raised the spectre of higher education information officers doing a poor job, and polytechnics, colleges and universities being perceived by adults as impenetrable. The responses to question 19 do not support this interpretation.

Confidence in Ability to Complete a Degree Course

Question 20: *On a scale of 1 to 5, are you confident that you could, if you so wished, successfully complete a degree course?*

Table 9.5: Confidence in Ability to Complete a Degree Course

	Parents	Applicants	Access	Friends	Total
1	15.2%	1.2%	3.1%	6.9%	6.6%
2	10.3%	2.9%	5.3%	6.2%	6.2%
3	20.8%	13.5%	27.6%	21.1%	20.7%
4	18.4%	34.1%	33.6%	27.1%	28.4%
5	35.2%	48.4%	30.3%	38.6%	38.1%
Average	3.48	4.26	3.82	3.84	3.85

It is interesting that Parents were, on average, the least confident that they could cope with a degree course, since a substantial proportion had already done so. This could perhaps be due to their greater average age than the other groups, or perhaps transmittal of nervousness on behalf of their children. A far higher proportion of Parents than other adults gave answers at the '1' or '2' level. The other groups demonstrated a significantly higher degree of confidence: only 8.5% expressed a less-than-average degree of confidence, while 67.4% said, in effect, that they were either 'confident' or 'very confident'. This further falsifies the view that adult application levels would be enhanced through an informational campaign indicating that adults can cope with degree-level study. Question 20, like question 19, tends to indicate that adults' limited understanding of higher education is less a matter of there being a poor flow of information about higher education, than limited interest in receiving such information.

Chapter 10   Analysis by Gender

As can be seen from **Table 10.1**, the majority of respondents, in all four categories, were female. The high preponderance of females in the Access categories can be taken to represent the relative gender balance in such courses. The preponderance of females in the Applicants categories, however, indicates a greater degree of co-operation from females approached than males: all things being equal, the proportions should have been 59.8% male, 40.2% female. The preponderance of females amongst the Parents and Friends categories is similarly interesting, and would seem to represent either a greater willingness of females than males to co-operate with surveys of this type, a greater propensity amongst sixth-formers to approach females than males for co-operation, or both.

Question 21: *Indicate whether you are male/female (circle one)*

Table 10.1: Gender Balance of Respondents

	Parents	Applicants	Access	Friends	Total
Male	45.0%	43.8%	30.6%	39.5%	39.8%
Female	54.8%	55.7%	68.0%	60.8%	59.5%
No answer	0.2%	0.4%	1.4%	0.7%	0.7%

In *Young People's Knowledge*, analysis of the answers by gender proved instructive: males gave more accurate answers to 'number' questions, such as those concerning the size and numbers of HEIs, while females gave more accurate answers to questions on practical issues such as availability of grants and minimum entrance requirements. The average responses from adults given below, however, follow a rather more monotonous pattern. With relatively few exceptions, the average male gave more accurate answers than the average female. This may be largely explicable by the fact that the average male adult was more likely to have experienced higher education than the average adult female. Analysis of question 16 by gender certainly supports such an explanation:

Question 16: *What is your highest level of academic qualifications achieved:*

Table 10.2: Highest Levels of Academic Qualifications Achieved

	Males	Females
1. No formal qualifications	10.9%	12.1%
2. O-levels or equivalent	26.5%	39.1%
3. A-levels or equivalent	36.2%	32.7%
4. HND or equivalent	10.2%	7.0%
5. Degree	16.2%	9.1%
No answer	0.3%	0.4%
Average answer (level)	2.94	2.62

As can be seen, participating males had achieved, on average, significantly higher levels of qualification than participating females, with 26.4% of males experiencing higher education, compared with 16.1% of females. This is wholly to be expected, since female under-representation at the higher levels of qualification has only recently been overcome. Since there would seem to be a greater propensity amongst traditional applicants to contact females in connection with information about higher education, it is fortunate that the level of direct knowledge of higher education amongst females will steadily increase in the coming years, as their increased participation feeds through into adult cohorts.

In view of the very high degree of competence shown by Parents in this questionnaire, their educational history was also analysed by gender. The following table shows that an extraordinary 57.4% of male Parents had experienced higher education—i.e. had gained qualifications at the level of the HND or equivalent or above. It cannot, of course, be deduced that 57.4% of all traditional applicants to higher education have a male parent with HND or above—there may be some element of special selectivity in this survey. (In fact the recent Heist survey of 5,858 potential applicants showed that 39% of respondents had at least one parent with a degree or similar—*Higher Education: The Student Experience.*) Only 38.7% of eligible parents completed the form, and it is possible, first, that parents with lower formal qualifications were less likely to complete the questionnaire. Second, males had a slightly lower propensity to complete the questionnaire than females, and it is possible that males that had experienced higher education were more likely than other males to participate. The figure of 57.4% might, therefore, somewhat flatter the male Parent category. It remains perfectly reasonable to conclude, however, that male parental possession of higher education qualifications is an exceedingly good indicator of likelihood, in the offspring, to apply for a higher education place.

Table 10.3: Parents' Highest Levels of Academic Qualification Achieved

	Males	Females
1. No formal qualifications	9.3%	13.8%
2. O-levels or equivalent	18.1%	36.2%
3. A-levels or equivalent	14.7%	18.9%
4. HND or equivalent	18.0%	12.4%
5. Degree	39.4%	18.6%
Average answer	3.59	2.86

Size and Number of HEIs

As can be seen from **Tables 10.4 and 10.5,** males gave more accurate answers than females on all 'size and number' questions. It is noticeable that males even gave more accurate answers with respect to CHEs, though these have been predominantly female in student make-up for some years.

Question 1: *Approximately how many British institutions of higher education are there in each main category?*

Table 10.4: Average Estimates of Numbers of HEIs

	Males	Females
Universities	80.9	106.1
Polytechnics	109.7	142.7
CHEs	216.1	234.6

Question 2: *On average, how many full-time students does each of the types of institution have?*

Table 10.5: Average Estimates of Size of HEIs

	Males	Females
Universities	4,010	3,890
Polytechnics	3,820	3,810
CHEs	2,630	2,910

Knowledge of Grants

The following tables give the proportions of males and females correctly stating what awards would be available at each type of HEI. As can be seen, males provide more accurate answers to all elements of all three questions, but not by so wide a margin as for the 'number and size' questions. It is worth recalling that sixth-form females significantly out-performed males on the 'streetwise' questions regarding grants and entrance qualifications.

Question 3: *Is a student grant automatically available (assuming you are British, have not previously received a grant, etc) to mature students for full-time degree courses in: [universities, polytechnics, colleges of higher education]*

Table 10.6: Availability of Mandatory Awards for Full-time Degree Courses

	Males	Females
Universities—yes	59.5%	55.8%
Polytechnics—yes	58.2%	54.2%
CHEs—yes	42.6%	40.3%

Question 4: *Is a DISCRETIONARY student grant available (i.e. if your local authority so chooses) to mature students for full time degree courses in: [universities, polytechnics, colleges of higher education]*

Table 10.7: Availability of Discretionary Awards for Full-time Degree Courses

	Males	Females
Universities—yes	84.3%	82.2%
Polytechnics—yes	85.5%	83.8%
CHEs—yes	78.1%	77.7%

Question 5: *Is a discretionary grant available (i.e. if your local authority so chooses) to mature students for PART-TIME degree courses in: [universities, polytechnics, colleges of higher education]*

Table 10.8: Availability of Discretionary Awards for Part-time Degree Courses

	Males	Females
Universities—yes	45.7%	43.0%
Polytechnics—yes	47.9%	43.3%
CHEs—yes	43.8%	40.8%

Nature of Courses

The next two tables give the average estimates, in years, of the length of courses. Again, males gave more accurate answers to the questions, but the difference was only significant in the case of the HND and HNC, where male knowledge was noticeably better.

Question 6: *What is the normal length of the following courses in England and Wales if taken on a full-time basis?*

Table 10.9: Normal Length of Courses Taken Full-time

	Male	Females
Degree	2.93	2.90
Honours degree	3.43	3.45
HND	2.37	2.51

Question 7: *What is the normal length of the following courses in England and Wales if taken on a PART-TIME basis?*

Table 10.10: Normal Length of Courses Taken Part-time

	Males	Females
Degree	4.41	4.38
Honours degree	5.06	5.11
HNC	3.39	3.64

Availability of Subjects at HEIs

Question 8, covering which subjects are available at the different types of HEI, showed some interesting variations between the genders. Overall, females gave slightly more accurate answers, with answers substantially more accurate for medicine, and noticeably more accurate for English, Secretarial Studies, and Philosophy. Males gave answers which were noticeably more accurate for Engineering and Business.

Entrance Requirements

The differences between the answers given by males and females to questions 9 and 10 were too small to merit summary in tables; females did, however, give very slightly more accurate answers than males to question 9, which concerned minimum entry requirements for full-time degrees, whereas males gave significantly more accurate answers to question 10, concerning minimum entry qualifications for a part-time degree course.

Proportions of Mature Students

Females gave significantly higher estimates than males of the numbers of mature students in higher education, as **Table 10.11** indicates. This was a move in the correct direction for part-time students, but in the wrong direction for full-time students.

Question 11: *What percentage of FULL-TIME students in British higher education is mature (i.e. aged 25 or over)?*

Question 12: *What percentage of PART-TIME students in British higher education is mature (i.e. aged 25 or over)?*

Table 10.11: Proportion of Students that are Mature (25 +)

	Males	Females
% of full-time students	14.35%	16.61%
% of part-time students	31.08%	32.63%

Standard of Degree Achieved by Mature Students

It is worth giving the full details of male and female responses to question 13, since the responses of the sexes differed quite markedly. In particular, females were very much more likely to state, correctly, that the average mature student gains a significantly better degree than those entering direct from school. One possible explanation is that the issue has received some attention from women's magazines.

Question 13: *The standard of degree achieved by mature students is, on average:*

Table 10.12: Standard of Degree Achieved by Mature Students

	Males	Females
1. Significantly below those entering direct from school	1.1%	1.2%
2. Slightly below those entering direct from school	8.7%	7.0%
3. About the same as those direct from school	21.7%	19.4%
4. Slightly better than those direct from school	47.0%	44.5%
5. Significantly better than those direct from school	20.6%	26.6%
Average answer	3.73	3.84

Question 14. *Name three actual British institutions in each of the following categories:*

Table 10.13: Numbers of HEIs Successfully Named

	Males	Females
Universities	2.74	2.60
Polytechnics	2.14	1.91
CHEs	0.44	0.39

As can be seen, males successfully named, on average, more HEIs in all three categories. The bare 'average' statistic does not disguise any interesting clusters: males gained higher scores than females in all categories, even—confirming the findings for questions 1 and 2—for CHEs, in which female participation has been high for many years.

Differential Preferences for HEIs Between the Sexes

The following two tables indicate the percentage of respondents including a particular university or polytechnic amongst their list of three. As usual, figures in brackets represent the 'league table' position. It should be remembered that males mentioned more HEIs than females, and thus the percentage figures for males are, in general, higher than those for females. Caution is necessary, therefore, in drawing conclusions about gender-preferences.

63

Table 10.14: Universities Named

	Male %	Female %
Aberystwyth	1.2% (40)	1.4% (38)
Aston	4.7% (21)	3.6% (23)
Bangor	1.6% (37)	1.6% (37)
Bath	4.6% (22)	4.0% (19)
Belfast	0.8% (44)	0.6% (43)
Birmingham	10.0% (8)	9.0% (8)
Bradford	2.6% (31)	2.9% (28)
Bristol	13.5% (4)	13.7% (5)
Brunel	2.0% (35)	1.6% (37)
Buckingham	0.1% (59)	0.1% (59)
Cambridge	29.4% (2)	32.3% (2)
Cardiff	5.0% (16)	4.9% (16)
City	0.4% (51)	0.6% (46)
Dundee	0.4% (53)	0.6% (48)
Durham	11.6% (6)	12.2% (6)
East Anglia	3.0% (28)	2.2% (32)
Edinburgh	4.9% (18)	4.7% (17)
Essex	1.9% (36)	1.9% (34)
Exeter	5.5% (14)	8.5% (9)
Glasgow	2.1% (34)	2.0% (33)
Heriot-Watt	0.8% (45)	0.4% (51)
Hull	5.6% (13)	5.2% (15)
Keele	5.5% (15)	3.8% (21)
Kent	3.5% (19)	4.2% (14)
Lampeter	0.6% (50)	0.1% (58)
Lancaster	4.1% (23)	3.6% (24)
Leeds	13.4% (5)	14.9% (3)
Liverpool	10.0% (9)	9.9% (7)
Loughborough	2.6% (30)	2.4% (30)
London	10.4% (7)	8.1% (10)

Table 10.14: Universities Named—*continued*

	Male %	Female %
Goldsmiths'	0.1% (57)	0.3% (53)
Holloway & Bedford	0.1% (56)	0.2% (54)
Imperial College	0.3% (55)	0.2% (57)
King's College	0.8% (44)	0.6% (47)
LSE	0.8% (46)	0.5% (49)
Queen Mary	0.2% (58)	0.2% (55)
UCL	0.9% (47)	0.7% (43)
Wye College	0.0% (60)	0.0% (60)
Manchester	15.5% (3)	14.4% (4)
UMIST	1.8% (37)	0.8% (41)
Newcastle	7.9% (10)	6.5% (13)
Nottingham	7.6% (11)	6.8% (12)
Open	0.2% (54)	0.1% (56)
Oxford	37.6% (1)	39.1% (1)
Reading	3.7% (24)	3.8% (22)
St Andrews	1.3% (41)	1.7% (36)
Salford	2.5% (32)	1.8% (35)
Sheffield	7.5% (12)	7.9% (11)
Southampton	3.5% (26)	3.4% (26)
Stirling	1.2% (40)	0.7% (42)
Strathclyde	0.6% (48)	0.4% (50)
Surrey	2.1% (33)	2.4% (31)
Sussex	4.7% (20)	3.6% (25)
Swansea	2.9% (29)	3.1% (27)
Ulster	0.4% (52)	0.3% (52)
York	4.9% (19)	5.3% (14)

As can be seen, males were distinctly more likely than females to mention Keele, Sussex, Newcastle and Warwick. Females showed a distinct preference for Exeter, and a rather less marked propensity to mention Bradford, Leeds, and Kent.

Table 10.15: Polytechnics Named

Polytechnic	Males	Females
Birmingham	10.0% (10)	9.9% (11)
Bournemouth	2.0% (32)	1.2% (32)
Brighton	7.7% (14)	7.2% (12)
Bristol	13.2% (6)	12.4% (7)
City of London	2.3% (30)	2.7% (29)
Coventry	6.5% (18)	5.2% (21)
East London	2.3% (31)	2.6% (30)
Hatfield	6.9% (16)	5.6% (19)
Huddersfield	5.5% (22)	5.5% (20)
Humberside	2.8% (29)	2.3% (31)
Kingston	7.3% (15)	7.0% (14)
Lancashire	6.8% (17)	5.0% (22)
Leeds	14.1% (3)	12.8% (5)
Leicester	7.9% (13)	6.6% (15)
Liverpool	13.8% (4)	13.4% (3)
Manchester	19.2% (1)	18.8% (1)
Middlesex	5.6% (21)	6.5% (16)
Newcastle	11.3% (9)	10.9% (9)
Nottingham	14.9% (2)	12.9% (4)
Oxford	13.1% (8)	12.7% (6)
PCL	4.7% (24)	3.2% (26)
PNL	5.9% (20)	5.9% (17)
Portsmouth	13.6% (5)	11.7% (8)
Sheffield	13.1% (7)	13.5% (2)
South Bank	4.3% (25)	4.2% (25)
South West	8.8% (11)	10.2% (10)
Staffordshire	5.0% (23)	4.5% (23)
Sunderland	8.4% (12)	7.1% (13)
Teesside	4.0% (26)	4.3% (24)
Thames	3.8% (27)	2.9% (28)
Wales	3.4% (28)	3.1% (27)
Wolverhampton	6.2% (19)	5.8% (18)

N.B. Bournemouth and Humberside had only recently been designated as polytechnics.

As can be seen, males showed a distinctly greater propensity to refer to Bournemouth, Lancashire, PCL, and Thames, while female preferences were to City of London, East London, Middlesex, South West, and Teesside.

Interest in Applying to HE

Table 10.16 shows that males and females felt equally likely to apply to a course at a university, but females expressed a greater propensity than males to apply for a polytechnic course.[21] This gives the lie, once again, to the notion that polytechnics are associated primarily with the engineering, science, and technical, courses, in which males predominate. **Table 10.16** would seem to indicate that females recognise, correctly, that females represent a higher proportion of students in the polytechnic sector than in the university sector.

Question 17: *On a scale of 1 to 5, are you at all likely to apply for a course in a university? (1 = not at all likely; 5 = extremely likely).*

Question 18: *On a scale of 1 to 5, are you at all likely to apply for a course in a polytechnic? (1 = not at all likely; 5 = extremely likely).*

Table 10.16: Likelihood to Apply for an HEI Course

	Males	Females
Q 17. Universities	2.56	2.56
Q 18. Polytechnics	3.06	3.13

Confidence about HE

Table 10.17 expresses the average answers given to the questions concerning the confidence of the respondents: confidence in being able, first, to find information about higher education, and confidence, secondly, in being able to complete a degree programme. As can be seen, males are on average rather more confident than females about finding information, and significantly more confident in their ability to complete a degree programme. The latter is fully consistent with the results of *Young People's Knowledge*. The higher levels of educational qualifications

[21] The figures represent the average answers, on a 1–5 scale, given. The averages do not disguise any interesting clusters.

achieved by adult males would no doubt partly explain their increased confidence. However, in the light of the increased confidence expressed by sixth-form males, whose education qualifications would be very similar to those of sixth-form females, it is likely that the adults' disparity is not explicable wholly in terms of qualification. As with many issues of gender, the disparity is chiefly of sociological significance.

Question 19: *On a scale of 1 to 5, are you confident of being able to find information about courses in higher education if you need it? (1 = not at all confident; 5 = very confident.)*

Question 20: *On a scale of 1 to 5, are you confident that you could, if you so wished, successfully complete a degree course? (1 = not at all confident; 5 = very confident.)*

Table 10.17: Confidence about HE

	Males	Females
Q 19. Ability to obtain information	4.14	4.07
Q 20. Ability to complete a degree course	4.02	3.75

Chapter 11   Conclusions and Recommendations

Table 11.1: Summary of Relative Knowledge of the Adult Groups

	Parents	Applicants	Access	Friends
Best answers given of 4 groups	21 times	9 times	1 time	1 time
Worst answers given of 4 groups	5 times	1 time	23 times	3 times

Access Students

Perhaps the clearest overall impression from the part of the survey covering 'right or wrong' questions must be the relative weakness of answers from Access students. **Table 11.1** shows just how marked this weakness was. Of the 32 main questions or sub-questions with right or wrong answers, Access students gave the most accurate answer just once (on the success of mature students), but the least accurate answer twenty-three times.

It must also be added that the weakness was not just relative. The quality of the answers was often disturbingly low, indicating that many Access students could be particularly ill-prepared to enter higher education. Examples are unfortunately numerous—they must include the belief by a quarter of the Access students that there are 500 or more British universities; the fact that only 36% knew the length of an honours degree; that 47% thought mandatory grants to be unavailable to adults for full-time degree study; and that only 52% thought that CHEs offer teacher training courses.

It is important to remember that most of the Access students were completing the questionnaire at the *beginning* of their programme, not at the end, and that their course could well address many of the misassumptions. It is clear, nevertheless, that the level of knowledge of higher education of those entering Access courses is so limited that the deficiency needs to be tackled vigorously, and from a number of directions. Access students themselves would seem to be in agreement with this, since they named by far the fewest sources of information about higher education, and readily admitted their paucity of information.

69

The first essential requirement in addressing the deficiency must be to ensure that its existence is well understood, both by Access course tutors and higher education admissions tutors. Access tutors, whose focus must be on the coursework, could easily assume that their students know much more about higher education than they do. Admissions tutors, also, are generally used only to the misassumptions of sixth-formers—they have substantial experience in correcting these, and are helped to do so by their institutions. In most cases, however, admissions tutors have little experience of correcting the misassumptions of adults. There is an inevitable tendency to assume that because such applicants *are* adults, they will know a lot more about the world, including higher education, than young people.

The publication reprinted in **Appendix One** is intended to make a useful contribution to the informational campaign. Its first printing of 75,000 met with an enthusiastic welcome, making an early reprinting necessary. But given the scale of the problem, such a publication cannot possibly suffice alone.

Individual HEIs could make a further important contribution by ensuring that the Access courses in their area are fully targeted for informational material. Such material must include prospectuses, leaflets, and—preferably—publications prepared specially for the audience, including an indication of where more information can be obtained. The most effective approach for HEIs might be to contact Access course tutors in their region to discover how many students are currently enrolled, and then deliver a package of information for each student. The package would perform not simply a valuable altruistic service: it would also win friends and increase application levels. CHEs, in particular, would benefit from the provision of such packs: they could use the opportunity to explain how the small ('more human') scale of the college, and its profile of courses, makes them particularly relevant to the adult applicant.

Access course tutors might wish to develop further the relationship with their local HEIs by inviting them to provide speakers, and developing, perhaps in partnership, course materials providing a reasonably synoptic overview of the nature of higher education. It is appreciated that syllabus time is limited, and that a substantial number of Access course students are not intending to enter higher education; nevertheless, an Access course would surely fail in one of its main objectives if it were to leave its students profoundly unaware of the institutions to which they are being given access. All Access courses should certainly ensure that a collection of higher education guides and other such publications is easily accessible to the students.

Access tutors and others would also perform a very useful service if they were to address the fact that Access students possessed the least under-standing amongst adults, by a considerable margin, of both HNDs and CHEs. As noted in earlier chapters, Higher National awards, and colleges of higher education, are in many ways of particular relevance to the 'back to study' audience: they provide respectively a course-type, and environment, which matches such students well. The CHEs would thus do well to consider individual or collective campaigns on this theme, while BTEC might target Access students directly through the course tutors.

Parents

Parents proved in some respects to be the mirror image of Access students, giving the best answers to 'right or wrong' questions far more often than any other.

The fact that Parents were so much more knowledgable than adult Applicants, and very often more knowledgable than sixth-form applicants, was one of the greater surprises of the survey. It might lead some to conclude that higher education can relax entirely about this group, and need not expend any effort on trying to improve their knowledge still further. It is arguable, however, that the Parents' level of knowledge is a clear indicator of their very high interest in higher education: perhaps demonstrating their own past involvement or that of their children.

An enterprising institution, agency, or sponsor might take note of the fact that the Parents' high level of interest is not reflected in the publications of higher education or its agents—very few attempts are made to address parents directly. A thoroughly useful public service could thus be performed by preparing a comprehensive 'Parent's Guide to Higher Education.' Such a guide might start off with general information about higher education, and might indicate that education should not 'stop' at a certain age, but it would focus particularly on those questions that most exercise parents: for example, questions about parental contributions to grants, about finding first-year accommoda-tion, about the employability of graduates, and about how higher education has changed since the parents had themselves left school. It could also usefully destroy fallacies, such as the pervasive fallacy about

71

there being a clear league of 'good' and 'bad' institutions. If the Guide showed how parents could genuinely help, and not hinder, their children (perhaps even giving tips on how not to embarrass them!) sixth-formers could be expected to convey the Guide to parents readily, minimizing distribution problems. A useful start in this direction has been made by both the Committee of Directors of Polytechnics and the Committee of Vice-Chancellors and Principals with their respective leaflets for parents.

Friends

The Friends could be considered, to some extent, a 'control' group. They did not have any particular connection with higher education, and could be considered reasonably representative of adults in the 25–35 age range. It was noticeable, in this context, that they were the weakest of all groups on questions about the availability of grants. In general, they thought that grants were not available to adults, with only 44.2% saying that mandatory awards were available to adults for full-time degree courses. This could be taken to indicate a widespread cultural assumption of those not in the direct 'need to know' brackets that grants exist to support school leavers only, and not older applicants. This is a serious misassumption that must be keeping many potential mature students from higher education.

Counteracting such a misassumption will not be easy, and will need to be addressed wherever the opportunity arises. Sections on grants for mature students could be added to prospectuses and other higher education materials, but of course this would tend to reach only those actively seeking information. Tackling others would be much more difficult, and action would probably need to be taken at DES level. Where the DES conducts specific recruitment campaigns, for example— such as the advertising campaign aimed at attracting people into teacher education (TASC)—it would do well to spread the message that grants are indeed available to adults.

Another cultural assumption demonstrated by the Friends, and which is likely to be at least as damaging as the assumption about grants, concerns the 'entry price' of higher education. 52.1% of Friends believed that A-levels or their equivalent were essential prerequisites, for adults, for acceptance onto a full-time degree course. Those lacking such qualifications, therefore, would assume that there would be no point whatever in their applying for such courses; it would not even be an aspiration.

This is another misassumption that, because it is so widespread amongst adult groups, will not be easy to overcome. Though the issue can be usefully addressed in the literature of HEIs, it is unlikely that the message would thereby reach most adults. Again, the only effective solution would seem to be an advertising campaign capable of gaining the attention of very large numbers of adults. Since such a campaign would be beyond the purse of individual HEIs, it would need to be carried out by the DES, or as part of a collective campaign. The experience of the Open University is encouraging: the OU successfully convinced many adults, through its advertising campaigns, that formal educational qualifications are *not* required for entry to its part-time degrees.

Applicants

Applicants stayed fairly well out of the limelight in the survey. On only one occasion was their average answer the weakest of the four groups, but they gave the best answer on only a modest number of occasions. It tends to be assumed that if an adult makes an application to higher education, then he or she will have put far more thought and research into it than a sixth-former, who might simply be fulfilling parental expectations or taking the line of least resistance. It may thus seem surprising that the Applicants' commitment and greater experience was not reflected in answers noticeably better than those of sixth-formers. On average, the Applicants' answers were in fact worse than upper sixth-formers, and only a little better than early lower-sixth-formers.

Those responsible for providing information about higher education need to be fully aware of this. It will be helpful to remember that while there is abundant help for the sixth-former, the adult applicant is left very much more to his or her own devices. The sixth-former will be enveloped in a higher education directed culture. There will be ready access to wall charts, higher education guides, teachers with knowledge of higher education, open day visits, etc, while friends will be similarly seeking entrance to higher education, and will thus be exchanging ideas and information. The adult applicant will lack nearly all of this. The sources of information that *are* available to adults thus become of greater individual importance. Those providing advice—such as admissions tutors and student services centres—need to be much more comprehensive in the information and services they make available.

A MATURE STUDENT'S GUIDE TO HIGHER EDUCATION

WHY READ THIS BOOKLET?

This booklet is written for adults who are thinking about taking a course in Higher Education be it in a polytechnic, a university or a college of higher education. We hope you will find if helpful whether you are just beginning to think about the option of Higher Education (HE), or whether you just want to know more about the HE system. The value of seeking professional advice at an early stage cannot be emphasized enough. Sources of information and advice are listed towards the end.

WHAT IS A MATURE STUDENT?

For the purposes of admission to Higher Education, a Mature Student is someone over the age of 21, who does not normally have the standard entry requirements. However different definitions are used for other purposes, for example for grants assessment, and the minimum age of 25 is often a key factor. These different definitions can be rather confusing.

Most students enter an HE institution with A levels or BTEC (Business and Technician Education Council) qualifications but under Mature Student regulations a polytechnic, university or college can consider an applicant who lacks these "normal" entry requirements, on the basis of their experience and/or alternative qualifications.

ABOUT HIGHER EDUCATION

Courses of Higher Education are offered in polytechnics, universities and colleges, and comprise the range of courses for which A level passes or their equivalent is the standard entry requirement. These include: degrees, BTEC Higher National Diplomas and Certificates, Diplomas of Higher Education, professional qualifications, and certain diplomas or certificates awarded by the institutions themselves. Many are offered both as full-time and part-time courses and some on a distance learning basis, the Open University in particular.

Under forthcoming legislation, polytechnics will be empowered to award their own degrees, and may, if they wish, adopt the title of university.

Degree Courses are offered at all three types of institution, in an enormous variety of both academic and vocational subjects. Students can opt for a single subject, joint subjects, or a degree in three or more combined subjects. Most full-time degree courses last for three years, with four years for a "sandwich" course, which includes one or more periods of practical experience within the time span of the course. This includes many technology and language courses, and some business and management courses. Many degrees can also be studied part-time, often over several years. "Extended" engineering or science courses are available. These are usually degrees incorporating a preliminary foundation year for those who cannot fulfil the traditional entry criteria.

The degree course structure is different in Scotland. Here the Pass or Ordinary degree course takes three years to complete, while the Honours course lasts normally four years or in a few cases (Modern Languages or enhanced Engineering degrees with work experience) five years.

BTEC Courses are offered at polytechnics and colleges, with the Higher National courses coming within the scope of Higher Education. BTEC (the Business and Technician Education Council) awards Certificates and Diplomas in a diverse range of vocational subjects, including agriculture, art and design, business studies, computing and engineering. A full-time Higher National Diploma course lasts for two years, and a sandwich course for three. Extended courses are also available with an initial foundation year for those without the traditional entry criteria.

Diploma of Higher Education (DipHE) courses are offered mostly at polytechnics and colleges. The full-time DipHE is a two year course equivalent to the first two years of a degree course. It is a broad-based programme of academic study, allowing for greater specialisation in the second year. The Diploma is a qualification in its own right or it can be used for entry to the third year of a related degree course. It was designed primarily for the needs of Mature Students who preferred not to commit themselves to a particular subject at the beginning of the course. Increasingly the DipHE is being used as a qualification for certain professional studies, notably social work and nursing.

Professional Qualifications are offered on a part-time or full-time basis mostly at polytechnics and colleges, and some other specialist providers (eg Hospital Schools of Radiography). They are validated by the appropriate professional body (for instance the Incorporated Society of Valuers and Auctioneers or the Institute of Chartered Accountants) which lays down the standards for entry and training in that profession. Courses are mostly at post A level standard and in some cases students may gain exemption from parts of the course on the basis of other qualifications, such as a BTEC HND or a Degree.

Institutions' Certificates and Diplomas are awarded by the individual college or polytechnic. They are offered in specialist vocational subjects usually related to the local industrial scene, for example Leicester Polytechnic's Certificate in Textiles.

WHY HIGHER EDUCATION WELCOMES MATURE STUDENTS

The typical Mature Student is frequently much better motivated, because (s)he knows just why (s)he wants to get the qualification, is usually a lot better at coping with organising study and social and family commitments than a school leaver and a lot less likely to be deterred by minor setbacks, and will work much harder. The Mature Student will typically ask more questions than the younger student, and get a good qualification. If you add this to demographic trends, with a reduction in the number of school leavers, you could be *very* welcome indeed to admissions tutors.

As the number of school-leavers falls, and the government seeks to expand the number of students in Higher Education, adults will become increasingly sought after by institutions of Higher Education. In 1990 the number of students aged 21 or over admitted through the Polytechnics Central Admissions System was 15447 to degree courses and 4514 to HNDs, and of these approximately 10% did not possess the standard entry requirement. Another feature in recent years has been the growth of 'Access' courses as an alternative route into Higher Education for the Mature Student.

It is true, however, that Mature Students are not evenly spread across all institutions and disciplines. A higher proportion of adults is to be found in Social Sciences and the Humanities than in Science and Technology. This is due partly to the students' own interests, but also to the fact that some subjects are more exacting in the precise subject knowledge required for entry. For example, a degree in Engineering generally requires a student to have studied A levels in Maths and Physics or a comparable subject, unless entering through the extended engineering route. It is also true that some institutions, departments and individual tutors are much more aware than others of the needs of mature students and also of the valuable contribution that an adult can make to a student group.

Anne is 34 years old and decided to return to education when her youngest child started school. Last year she took a GCSE in English Language at evening classes, and was delighted to obtain a grade A. She went on to enrol for an Access course at her local Further Education College. She was hoping to obtain a place on a Social Work course, but was not accepted because she had insufficient experience. However she has been offered a place on a Social Sciences degree course at her local polytechnic. She is happy to accept this and hopes to continue on to Social Work training at the end of the course.

Vivienne is 36 and is a qualified State Registered Nurse, working in a large teaching hospital. She started an Open University course in Social Sciences two years ago, as her work patterns (changing shifts) made attendance at a regular class difficult. She enjoyed the course immensely and decided that she would like to change to a full-time course if that was possible. She was accepted on to a Psychology degree course at a College of Higher Education, and having investigated the financial implications, she has decided to resign from her job and start the course in the following September. She isn't sure what she wants to do at the end of the course, but is not unduly worried at this stage!

Gary is 24 and works in the Information Technology Department of a large manufacturing company. He was employed by the company when he left college with a BTEC National Diploma, and now works as a Junior Programmer. He enjoys the work and the pay is good, but he feels he needs to obtain higher qualifications in order to progress to more senior posts within the industry. He has therefore applied for a Higher National Diploma course in Computer Studies.

DO I WANT TO BE A STUDENT?

Your decision about whether to become a student depends on what you want, whether Higher Education can offer you something suitable, and your circumstances.

There are many valid reasons for becoming a student:

*   to develop further your existing skills and knowledge, building upon all the learning you have acquired to date - in your job, as a homemaker and parent, in voluntary work, or from spare time interests;

*   to make an entirely fresh start, in an area you haven't previously studied but in which you are interested. This may give you the opportunity for a change of direction in your life;

*   to get appropriate qualifications for your career;

*   for personal development, by stretching yourself and using your mind to tackle a higher level course of study, and personal satisfaction from the challenge it offers you;

*   to study a subject because you enjoy it!

George had worked in banking all his life. When he left the bank after a serious illness, he decided to have a complete change. He is now studying for a B.A. Humanities in History and Spanish.

Ann is a single parent. Following her divorce, the challenge of higher education is giving her a new sense of her own value, and the Law course will lead to good employment prospects as well as being an interesting subject. She is representing her polytechnic in the lawyers' client counselling competition.

Chris has been working in an engineering company since he left school. He now wants to take a degree in electronic engineering, extending his understanding and qualifying him for professional engineer status.

Whatever your reasons for returning to study it is important that, taking as much advice as possible, you fully assess yourself – your abilities, interests, values, benefits and motivations – and consider the many learning opportunities which are available to you. If you really *want* to be a student, if you know you are on the right course to lead to your chosen outcome, then you are much more likely to succeed.

It is also important that you consider how becoming a student fits in with your other plans and circumstances. Will you find time to study? Will you get a grant and student loan? Can you commit yourself to two, three, or more years of study (and if not, will you be able to take a break and transfer credit for the work you have done)? If you know you have thought this through, you will be more confident that you are taking the right step.

You may well find it valuable to talk through your ideas with advisory staff at an Educational Guidance Service for Adults, in the local Careers Service or in the Student Service Centre at your local HE institutions.

CAN I BE A STUDENT?

Will I have the entry requirements?
Many Mature Students worry about getting GCSE and A level passes to gain entry to courses in Higher Education. This can take a very long time, and may not be the best route for you.

Appendix 1

Admissions tutors do not need to ask mature students for the same formal qualifications that are expected from school leavers, though in some cases they will do so. In order to exempt you from these, they will be looking for evidence of:

*   ability to study

*   some study at the same level as BTEC National or A level

*   relevant background or preliminary knowledge/skills, for study in some subject areas (eg Maths or a numerate subject for Science and Engineering).

You will need to find the best way to present evidence of these to the admissions tutor. It may be that your current or previous employment or voluntary work will provide this, without additional study. On the other hand, even if you meet all the formal entry requirements, you may wish to undertake some preparatory studies to boost your confidence about studying, especially if it is many years since you last took a formal course.

> *Jaswinder had A levels when she left school ten years ago. While she was offered entry to the polytechnic on the basis of these, she chose to take a short "Prepare to Study" course to reassure herself that she could cope with study. She met other mature students, making friends she continues to see now she is on her degree course, and gained confidence.*

Preparatory study
In many areas, there are opportunities to take courses which will help you prepare for your return to study and/or to gain entry qualifications before you take a degree or diploma course. "Access", "Return to Study", "PolyPrep" or similar courses may be offered specifically for adults who are returning to HE by local Further Education Colleges and Adult Education Centres, or by the polytechnics, universities and colleges themselves. These may be offered as full-time or part-time learning programmes. You may, alternatively, take distance or open learning packages or work independently to improve your study skills and background knowledge and as preparation for student life. Which you choose will depend on your own preferences, on what is available in your own area, and on the requirements of the institution you wish to attend.

> *Peter is 39 years old. He worked as an engineering fitter but was made redundant when his company closed down five years ago. He had always been active in his Trade Union branch, and when he lost his job became involved in the town's Unemployment Centre. He also joined classes run by the local branch of the Workers Education Association (W.E.A.). His tutor told him about courses run by the Adult Residential Colleges, and he was accepted on a two year Liberal Studies course. He has just started a course in Modern History at polytechnic, and would like to go on to teach in Adult Education.*

You can get help in choosing what will suit you from an Educational Guidance Service for Adults, Careers Service or from advisory staff at your local polytechnic, university or college.

Can I get credit for prior experience and learning?

If you already have directly relevant qualifications or experience, there is the possibility that these may be accepted as equivalent to sections of the new course and that you will be given credit for them, therefore avoiding having to repeat the same study. In some cases there may be well-established criteria for equivalence, but it may involve an assessment process for which you may have to pay. If it is your experience that you want taken into account, then the process will be one in which you demonstrate your skills and knowledge. This is not yet widespread, but is expected to become more common.

If you think that you would be eligible for this, talk to an adviser about "accreditation of prior (and prior experiential) learning". Even if you don't get credit or exemption your prior knowledge and experience will make your further study much easier, and will allow you to concentrate on new areas of study.

Susan is 36 years old and has three children. She got three O levels at school, and took two more at evening classes in the last few years. Before having her children she had done clerical work in a bank and a large commercial office. More recently she has worked as a Foster Parent and a Care Assistant. In addition to in-service training for these jobs she has taken a range of part-time classes over the years, including Office Skills and Computing, Local History and a New Opportunities course. She has also been actively involved in voluntary work.

Last year she applied for an Access course in Health Studies, for which students are mainly assessed on the basis of previous experience (Accreditation of Prior Experiential Learning). She was accepted on the basis of both her paid and voluntary work experience, educational qualifications and her experience in the home and family. Susan obtained Distinctions or Merits in all subjects and has just started a degree in Podiatric Medicine (Chiropody).

Am I too old?

A common question, it is partly answered by the statistics. In 1986 a quarter of all first year full-time students were mature, an increase of 23% since 1979. There was an increase of 54% in mature part-time students over the same period - the number of women in this group nearly doubled. Eighty three percent of Mature Students are in colleges and polytechnics (figures from Labour Market Quarterly, January 1989). So when you become a Mature Student at college, polytechnic, or university, you will be joining a growing band returning to education after a period in employment, bringing up a family, or some other break.

You are never too old to benefit from studying a new subject, and from the personal development and satisfaction that results. However, if you intend that your study should lead to a new career, then age may be a factor in recruitment, and you should ask the careers advisory service at whichever polytechnics, universities or colleges you are considering to tell you both about general employment prospects and the success of mature students in particular. Demographic trends should increase your employment prospects considerably, but you may well have to sell the positive aspects of a mature recruit to some employers. You will be offered plenty of help by advisory staff.

> *Peter was 59 years old when he first approached the Education Advice Service. He had been unemployed for six years following a long illness, and was not hopeful of finding work in the near future. He had a life-long interest in mathematics, but did not feel ready to undertake a full-time course at that stage. Peter started attending an O level maths class at a Community Education centre, and after six months, encouraged by the tutor, he applied for the Open University. After a year with the OU, he came back to the Advice Worker to discuss the possibility of a full-time course. She put Peter in touch with the Maths Department at the local polytechnic, and he is now in his third year of a combined degree in Maths and Computing.*

Will I cope?

You need to be sure that you have all the necessary skills to organise your time, take notes, read effectively, and write essays and reports. You also need to be sure that you can cope with the level of work required on the course. Many students will have proved to themselves that they already have the ability from appropriate previous studies, but you may equally have demonstrated these skills through employment, voluntary work or leisure activity. Otherwise, as a start, consider preparatory study of some kind.

> *Jane came to the student adviser in her second term to discuss her work. She had not handed in any essays, and had missed deadlines, because she felt they were not quite right yet. She was afraid that they would not be good enough. Talking with the student adviser, she realised she was doing well, collecting appropriate information, planning her essays, and presenting her assignments well - but she just needed to find this out! She now has the confidence to produce work and hand it in on time.*

Can I afford it?

If you are considering studying at polytechnic, university or college, one of your major considerations will be finance. Your eligibility for an award, how much you will receive, and any contributions from spouse (or parents), will therefore be crucial.

Within the regulations, an award is defined as comprising both the fee element, and the maintenance element while a grant refers only to the maintenance element, which is means-tested. If you are eligible for an award, your fees will be paid directly by your LEA to your institution and your grant (if any) will be paid to you to cover term-time and the short vacations.

Mandatory grants are paid as of right to students who follow "designated" courses and satisfy the qualifying conditions, including residence. Designated courses include first degree, HND, DipHE, BEd/PGCE, and other Certificates and Diplomas comparable at least to first degrees provided by an HE institution. If you do not qualify for a mandatory grant or are not intending to take a designated course you may still qualify for a discretionary grant, which could be up to the same level. LEAs have individual policies on these.

Your grant is means tested, either on your own income or your spouse's or your parents'. If you will be over 25 years before the start of your course or have been self-supporting from earnings three years before your course begins, or were married at least two years before the start of your course, or both your parents are dead, or you are a single parent, then you will be regarded as having "independent status" and the parental contribution will not be assessed. Earned income during the year (including vacations) will not affect your grant. It will however count towards your income tax allowance. Unearned income in excess of specified limits may reduce your grant.

You may get additional allowances as a Mature Student. If you are aged 26 years or over and have earned or received (in benefits) a certain specified sum during the three years before the start of the course, there is an Older Students Allowance. You may receive dependants' allowances for your spouse and your children. (However, any income they receive may affect their status.) For more information the Department of Education and Science booklet "Grants to Students – a brief guide" is available from your LEA or the Student Services of your local HE institution, local education authority or careers office.

From 1990, financial support for students has included a loan element. This has meant:

* the freezing of grants and parental contributions in cash terms at the present level;

* a loan facility of about £1600 over a three year course at 1992/3 levels;

* the removal of Housing Benefit, Unemployment Benefit and Income Support from students (except students who are disabled or single parents, and dependents on or partners of students, who will still be able to claim benefits).

Timetable for Loans

Autumn 1990   Grants increase by 3.5%.
                   Loans available to all British full-time students, including those part-way through their courses. (Housing Benefit, Unemployment Benefit and Income Support no longer available to students.)
Autumn 1991   Grants frozen
to Autumn 2007 Loans increased annually by an amount reflecting inflation rate.
Post 2007   Loans estimated to have reached 50% of a student's upkeep. Grants and loans, from then on, index-linked.

A higher loan is available during early years of the course which include a long vacation, and is lower in the final year.

Students will be allowed nine months after their course ends before they must begin repayments, or longer if their income remains less then 85% of average earnings. The loans will be interest-free (in real terms) with outstanding debt up-rated in line with inflation, and will probably have to be repaid within five years.

Linda is 33 and has been working in an accounts/admin job for sixteen years. She had not done any studying since leaving school until last year when she took and passed a GCSE in English. She feels that she is in a rut at work, and

> *would like to study in Higher Education to open up new career prospects. Linda is single and has recently bought a flat. When she looked carefully at the financial implications she decided that she would be unable to give up her job and survive on a grant, and that she would prefer to consider part-time courses. She has enrolled on an A level evening course, and intends to apply for the part-time degree in Law next year*

Your total resources will therefore include your grant, any contribution from your spouse (or parents) plus any additional allowances. Single parents, and handicapped students, are the only categories of students who may in addition claim benefits.

This may sound complicated! It is a good idea to talk through your financial position with your adviser, or the awards section of your local education authority. Do this before you commit yourself to a course, to make sure that you know your position. Two booklets from the Department of Education and Science are "essential reading" on this topic: "Grants to Students - a brief guide" and "Loans for students - a brief guide", both of which are revised annually. For advice to students in Scotland and Northern Ireland, the Scottish Education Department and Department of Education for Northern Ireland also produce guidance.

Remember that a few years on low income may result in substantial rewards, both monetary (with graduates earning higher pay on average) and in terms of personal satisfaction and achievement but as is suggested below this is not guaranteed.

Too many mature students feel that their future will be assured once they have a degree, and, sadly, that is not always the case. Apart from those who find it difficult to gain employment, there are others who have to begin at a salary lower than the one which they left, particularly if they enter a field in which they have no prior experience or one which, like social work, is simply a poorly rewarded profession.

What about family and friends?
It isn't only you who will be affected by your return to study. As you develop personally, your family and friends will notice the change in you, and your relationships with them will change. Do think about how they will cope with this, and also accept that some friendships may be outgrown in the process. There is also the practical aspect of the demands that family and friends will make on you when you are a student - you may need to be firm with them in setting aside time for study when family and friends are not welcome. The availability of childcare facilities may be of practical importance. You should discuss your needs with Student Services staff at your chosen institution, and make quite sure that the available childcare allows you to devote sufficient time to study.

You will meet many new people and make new friends as a student: when the time comes for you to graduate, your family and friends, both old and new, will share in your achievement.

Housing
Many Mature Students attend their local polytechnic, university or college because of other, (especially family), commitments. If however, you are intending

to move away to study, you will need to look at the accommodation available and what it is likely to cost. This will vary considerably from one institution to another. Some will provide accommodation, others will rely mainly on the private sector for rented housing, in bed-sits, flats or shared houses. The Accommodation Office of each polytechnic, university or college will be able to provide information. There may be Halls of Residence, but they are principally allocated to 18 year-olds and overseas students away from home for the first time. It could be great fun – or simply very wearing! If you need accommodation for you and your dependants then you should start looking very early, as you may also have to consider other factors, such as schooling. Remember that most students do not have dependants and that institutions may not own or have access to family accommodation.

With the introduction of student loans, students' entitlements to housing benefit have been abolished and the cost of accommodation may well be the key determinant in your choice of where you study.

WHAT COURSE? WHERE DO I DO IT?

If you would like to enter Higher Education, you will want to start to make some decisions about which course best meets your requirements and where it would be best to study it.

The merest glance at what is available will show a vast range of possibilities with an ever growing number of course and subject combinations available in an increasing range of attendance patterns.

So, how do you decide for which courses to opt? There are no hard and fast rules for making these choices, but you should take many factors into consideration.

WHICH SUBJECT DO I STUDY?

Will the subject give me scope for personal development?
Although this is a bit hazy and will very clearly mean something different for everyone, it is important and in the long-term might be the most significant aspect of taking an HE course. You might want to think about courses in terms of the extent to which they will build things like your self-confidence, your conceptual skills, your ability to understand yourself and your environment, your personal relationships or your non-academic skills.

Will the subject enhance my employment possibilities?
Statistical evidence shows that the more advanced your qualifications, the more likely you are to find better paid, more satisfying work, although of course that isn't a guarantee! Sometimes older graduates have proceeded to take Masters degrees or PhDs because they had difficulty in gaining employment after a first degree, only to find that for many jobs they are regarded as "overqualified" and "over-aged". Likewise, some older graduates with first class honours degrees are considered, usually unjustly, by employers to be too academic.

Much depends on the graduate's degree discipline, its relevance to the career to which entry is sought and to the graduate's previous work and life experience. Research has shown that employers are more willing to stretch age limits for applicants whose previous experience and degree subject are relevant than for others who cannot show such relevance.

If you have a specific employment goal, then there may be a specific course you need to take. Vocational courses are likely to be popular with applicants of all ages and admissions tutors may prefer good grades at A level or Highers to the alternative entry route of Access courses or giving you credit for prior learning. Do seek advice at the earliest possibility.

There are more likely to be a number of different routes to your vocational goal, so it will often pay to look beyond the obvious courses. You might, for example, want to consider taking a joint or combined course rather than a single subject course in order to broaden your options, but do check that the chosen course does actually enable you to enter your preferred employment area.

If you don't have any firm ideas about what employment area you wish to go into, don't panic. Most people do not have firm ideas, or, if they had at the start of the course, they have often changed their minds by the time they finish it. Each year thousands of graduates enter employment in areas that are totally unrelated to what they studied. Certainly give thought to the vocational outcomes of a particular course, but don't feel pressured to make decisions before you need to. Most HE Careers Services encourage mature students to use their services before their final year.

Which course will I enjoy?
For many mature entrants this might appear to be a luxurious question to ask, after a period of work, child-rearing or unemployment. However, if you are about to spend the next few years in Higher Education during which time you will be expected to be self-motivated in the face of a whole range of pressures and difficulties, then our strong advice to you is to choose a subject that you will enjoy.

It might be something you enjoyed at school (although remember that many of the subjects available in Higher Education are not taught in school), or be an interest you have developed since then or something you have had a hankering to do but not the opportunity. Look at all the alternatives that you think you might enjoy and find out more about them.

If you don't reach any very definite conclusions about subjects, again do not worry. More and more places are offering the opportunity to study a broad range of subjects in the first year of a course and then to specialise later, while others also offer courses that enable you to "pick and mix" from a range of optional modules.

What is the content of the course?
While courses share the same name they can vary enormously in content. So, having broadly decided which subject or subjects you might wish to study, have a look at what the courses cover and whether they meet your requirements. What is

the balance between different parts of the course? Are there any compulsory elements in the course? What opportunities exist to change track or transfer if it proves not to be suitable?

What learning methods does the course use?
A majority of courses place considerable emphasis on a student's ability to learn independently. Most arts and social science courses use a mixture of lectures, seminars and tutorials; more technical and scientific courses will place more emphasis on workshops. The more practical the subject, the more practical the learning will tend to be, with a greater emphasis on "doing" rather than "discussing".

In recent years there has been an increasing emphasis on "experiential" learning (ie learning through experience or doing) in all subjects.

It might be worth finding out if information is available from an institution on the average group size for each learning activity on your proposed course.

What assessment methods will be used?
The trend in recent years has been away from traditional examinations and towards continuous assessment and assignment-based assessment. In association with this, an increasing number of courses are basing assessment on the previous experience of students and enabling Mature Students to be credited for previous work and qualifications. This development is patchy but worth checking out.

What percentage of students on the course are mature?
Experience indicates that Mature Students perform best when they constitute at least a sizeable minority on the course. You will find that on some courses Mature Students may form a majority of the total number of students.

Do study skills form part of the course?
If you have been out of formal education for a while, you will probably find it useful to be able to take a study skills option which will help you to get back into the swing of studying again. Find out if a course or help is provided and whether you will be credited for any work you do in this area.

WHICH POLYTECHNIC, UNIVERSITY OR COLLEGE SHALL I GO TO?

For many Mature Students this is not an option - because of your circumstances you will have already decided that you will have to go to the nearest one. If you can only attend one, remember that you can still choose four courses at that institution when applying through PCAS and/or five courses through UCCA.

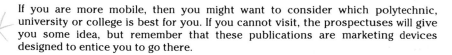

If you are more mobile, then you might want to consider which polytechnic, university or college is best for you. If you cannot visit, the prospectuses will give you some idea, but remember that these publications are marketing devices designed to entice you to go there.

Institutions may be city-based, possibly spread across several sites, or can be some distance from the nearest town centre. There will be significant differences in the range of services and facilities on offer to students, in terms of support, childcare and medical resources, and also sports and recreational facilities.

Does the course involve travel between sites?
In recent years many polytechnics, universities and colleges have expanded into additional premises. Consequently, this can involve considerable travel between sites. Find out what sort of distances are involved and whether free and frequent transport is provided.

Is childcare provided?
With the increasing number of Mature Students, many institutions now provide childcare facilities. Find out if there is a charge and whether it is available on-site or away from where you will be studying.

What facilities are provided for people with disabilities?
Like the childcare facilities, this is not only of interest if you have a disability yourself but in general terms it will also give you an indication of the attitude of the institution towards its students.

MAKING YOUR APPLICATION

If you wish to apply for a full-time or sandwich degree, DipHE or HND course at a polytechnic you must apply through PCAS. Applications for full-time and sandwich degree courses at university are made through UCCA. Applications for these courses at colleges of higher education are mostly made through PCAS but some colleges of higher education recruit through UCCA. Before applying you must obtain an application form and a copy of the PCAS *Guide for Applicants* and the UCCA *Handbook*. Although both organisations run separate application procedures they operate a single, combined application form.

(Applications for part-time courses are made direct to the institutions.)

Essentially PCAS and UCCA act as a post box between you, as the applicant, and the institutions to which you have applied. They do not intend to come in the way of direct contact between you and the polytechnics, universities or colleges but they are keen to ensure that fair, consistent and easily understood procedures are observed by applicant and institutions alike.

Further details about applications procedures, and application forms are available from:

UCCA/PCAS, PO Box 67, Cheltenham, Glos GL50 3SF

Applications should ideally be made between 1 September and 15 December in the year prior to entry. Many mature applicants do not make their minds up until well after that date, and applications can continue to be made until courses start in September/October. The main problem with later applications is the availability of places on the more popular courses: although mature applicants are welcome at any time, admissions tutors may have very few, if any, places left on high-demand courses.

After you have applied, PCAS and/or UCCA will guide you through the procedures one stage at a time. Consult a careers adviser, or PCAS or UCCA, if you are in any doubt as to your options. If concerned about the appropriateness of your background, contact the admissions tutor for the course in advance of your application.

Take care with your application. Admissions tutors may well wish to interview you, but this is your first, and possibly your only, opportunity to impress.

SOURCES OF ADVICE

Educational guidance services for adults (EGSAs)
These are free and independent services that will assist you in finding out more, discussing what you require and how best you can do what you want to do. They will have the standard reference books and guides as well as prospectuses and course leaflets. They are used to dealing with adults and should be able to understand how you feel and what your situation is like. Not all areas have a service, but your local library will be able to tell you if one exists near you. The National Association for Educational Guidance for Adults publishes a national directory each Autumn for those in England and Wales (costing £2.50 and available from the address overleaf).

Careers services
Many Local Education Authority (LEA) Careers Services offer an information and advice service specifically for adults broadly similar to the EGSA's. Find out how your local careers service can help.

Although the primary role of Careers Services in Higher Education is to help their own students and graduates, an increasing number are happy to offer advice to the would-be applicant. Students on Access Courses in Further Education Colleges can usually avail themselves of the advice and information from the Careers Service on site.

Careers Services throughout the United Kingdom have the advantage of a very large network of local offices, most with careers information libraries. Details are given in telephone directories under "Careers Service". Some institutions have established guidance services that aim to ease the path into Higher Education and offer advice on what to apply for and how to apply for it. Otherwise most admissions tutors will be prepared to advise on applications.

Further education and adult education staff
If you are currently taking a course in further or adult education, your tutor should be a good source of assistance and information.

Library
Your local reference library will contain many of the sources of information you require and may have staff who will be able to help you.

Appendix 1

ADDRESSES

PCAS (Polytechnics Central Admissions System)
Fulton House
Jessop Avenue
Cheltenham
Gloucestershire
GL50 3SH

UCCA (Universities' Central Council on Admissions)
PO Box 28
Cheltenham
Gloucestershire
GL50 3SA

NAEGA (National Association for Educational Guidance for Adults)
c/o Anne Docherty
The Mews Cottage
7 Botanic Crescent Lane
Glasgow
G20 8AA

Jasbinder arrived at her local Educational Guidance Service and announced that she had been to see "Educating Rita" and that she had decided that she would like to take a degree.

Over a number of months, Jasbinder made a number of visits to the Guidance Service. Initially she was very uncertain about what she wanted to study: she just knew that she had to escape from a job that she found boring and had come to hate.

The Service's staff worked with her in order to identify which course she would like, which she could do, where she could do it, how to apply for the courses she had chosen, how to get a grant and how to survive financially; and to give a regular confidence boost everytime she had convinced herself that she could not go through with it.

She has recently completed a Humanities degree and has applied successfully to do a Youth and Community Work course, following the part-time work she did in a Community Centre while taking her degree. She is waiting to hear if she will receive a grant to do the course.

BOOKLIST

A number of suggested books and directories are listed below, many of which will be available for reference in careers offices, libraries and institutions, as well as in bookshops.

Choice of course
Heap: **YOUR CHOICE OF DEGREE.**
Easy to read introduction to subject choices.

Bell, Hamilton, Roderick: **MATURE STUDENTS ENTRY TO HIGHER EDUCATION**
Guide for adults wishing to enter Higher Education, mainly at degree level.

Pates, Guide: **SECOND CHANCES.**
Guide to the full range of education and training opportunities for adults.

Rosier, Earnshaw: **MATURE STUDENTS HANDBOOK**
Guide for adults interested in Higher Education including career implications.

Careers Research Advisory Council: **DEGREE COURSE GUIDES.**
Detailed guide to individual degree course subjects, allowing students to compare aspects such as teaching and assessment methods, course content and options, selection procedures, etc.

Newpoint Publishing Company: **WHICH DEGREE?**
Five volumes listing degree courses by subject, and providing institutions, including entry requirements and course content.

Guides to courses and entry requirements

Polytechnics Central Admissions System: **GUIDE FOR APPLICANTS.**
Guide to courses within the PCAS scheme.

Committee of Directors of Polytechnics: **POLYTECHNIC COURSES HANDBOOK**
The official guide to full-time advanced courses in polytechnics, including entry requirements. A separate **POLYTECHNIC COURSES LEAFLET** is also published annually listing all full-time and sandwich courses available in polytechnics.

Council for National Academic Awards: **DIRECTORY OF FIRST DEGREE AND DIP HE COURSES.**
Guide to advanced courses validated by the CNAA.

Regional Advisory Councils: **COMPENDIUM OF ADVANCED COURSES IN COLLEGES OF FURTHER AND HIGHER EDUCATION.**
Guide to advanced courses in colleges and polytechnics.

Standing Conference of Principals: **COLLEGES AND INSTITUTES OF HIGHER EDUCATION: 1991 GUIDE.**
Guide to full and part-time courses in this sector.

NATFHE: **THE HANDBOOK OF INITIAL TEACHER TRAINING, COURSES IN INSTITUTES/COLLEGES OF HE, POLYTECHNICS AND UNIVERSITY DEPARTMENTS OF EDUCATION IN ENGLAND AND WALES.**
A detailed guide to courses leading to qualified teacher status.

Higgins, Lamley: **HOW TO COMPLETE YOUR UCCA/PCAS FORM:**
Trotman and Company.
Step by step guidance on completing the application form.

Appendix 1

Universities Central Council on Admissions: **UCCA HANDBOOK**
Applicants guide to applying through the UCCA system ie first degree courses at
Universities.

Sheed and Ward: **UNIVERSITY ENTRANCE**.
The main guide to University entrance, including entry requirements.

ECCTIS 2000.
On-line database of Access and Higher Education courses - terminals in many
careers offices.

ECCTIS: **ACCESS TO HIGHER EDUCATION COURSES DIRECTORY**.
Guide to UK Access or Preparatory Courses.

ECCTIS: **STUDENTS' GUIDELINES TO EDUCATIONAL CREDIT TRANSFER**

ECCTIS: **EDUCATIONAL CREDIT TRANSFER, ECCTIS HANDBOOK**
Guide to current arrangements for recognition of previous study for entry to and
movement within the Higher Education system.

Trotman and Company: **GETTING INTO POLYTECHNIC, GETTING INTO
UNIVERSITY and GETTING INTO COLLEGE**.
Three slim books giving tips on how to approach and prepare for the application.

Art and Design Admissions Registry: **COURSES IN ART AND DESIGN**.
Applicants' guide to courses in art and design.

Dalebank Books: **POTTER GUIDE TO HIGHER EDUCATION**.
A researched guide to the HE institutions in PCAS and UCCA, covering aspects of
their environment, accommodation, locality and travel.

Careers Research Advisory Council: **STUDENT EYE**.
Guide to Higher Education Institutions as seen by the students.

Heap: **DEGREE COURSE OFFERS**.
Information about degree course offers made to applicants in the previous year.

Kogan-Page: **BRITISH QUALIFICATIONS**.
Describes education establishments, accrediting and examining bodies, covering
Higher Education, vocational and professional education. Plus a useful list of
abbreviations.
British Council: **INTERNATIONAL GUIDE TO QUALIFICATIONS IN BRITAIN**.
Guide to overseas qualifications, by country, including British equivalent, marking
systems and structure of the education system.

Grants

DES: **GRANTS TO STUDENTS: A BRIEF GUIDE**.
Information on Mandatory Awards for students in Higher Education.

DES: **LOANS FOR STUDENTS; A BRIEF GUIDE**.
Information on the new student loans scheme.

Education Grants Advisory Service, NUS, UK Council for Overseas Student Affairs: **MONEY TO STUDY**.
Authoritative guide to sources of both statutory and non-statutory financial help. For further information contact EGAS at 501–5 Kingsland Road, Dalston, London E8 4AU.

Northern Ireland Department of Education: **GRANTS TO STUDENTS, A BRIEF GUIDE**.
Available free of charge from your local Education and Library Board or from the Department of Education, Scholarship Branch, Rathgael House, Balloo Road, Bangor, Co Down BT19 2PR.

Scottish Education Department: **GUIDE TO STUDENTS ALLOWANCES**.
Available free of charge from the Scottish Education Department, Gyleview, 3 Redheughs Rigg, South Gyle, Edinburgh EH12 9HH.

Employment Prospects

AGCAS: **WHAT DO GRADUATES DO?** Hobson Publishing.
Provides a comprehensive picture on graduate employment trends with a statistical analysis of the destinations of mature graduates.

AGCAS: **MATURE STUDENTS – WHAT'S NEXT?**
Practical job seeking for mature students.

AGCAS: **SURVEY OF EMPLOYER ATTITUDES TOWARDS THE RECRUITMENT AND EMPLOYABILITY OF OLDER GRADUATES**.

Graham: **OLDER GRADUATES AND EMPLOYMENT**.
Extensive report on age discrimination by employers.

Graham: **MESSAGES FROM MATURE GRADUATES**.

Note This leaflet is also published as part of a book entitled *Adults' Knowledge of Higher Education* (C N Keen and M A Higgins) published by the Higher Education Information Services Trust and PCAS. It has been written by Chris Cooper, Jane Barret and Paul Cave of the National Association for Educational Guidance for Adults and Alison Foster of PCAS.

Appendix 2 The Questionnaire

The Nature of Higher Education

*Please answer **each** of the following questions. We realise that you are unlikely to know the answers to a number of the questions, but please do not skip any—give your best guess on each occasion.*

A. Types of Higher Education Institution

1. *Approximately how many British institutions of higher education are there in each main category (**tick one number in each row**).*

	30	40	60	80	100	200	300	500	800
Universities									
Polytechnics									
Colleges of HE									

2. *On average, how many full-time students does each of the types of institution have (**tick one number in each row**).*

	1,000	2,000	3,000	4,000	6,000	8,000
Colleges of HE						
Polytechnics						
Universities						

B. Grants

3. *Is a student grant automatically available (assuming you are British, have not previously received a grant etc) to mature students for full-time degree courses in:*

Polytechnics	yes/no **(circle one)**
Colleges of HE	yes/no **(circle one)**
Universities	yes/no **(circle one)**

4. *Is a DISCRETIONARY student grant available (ie. if your local authority so chooses) to mature students for full-time degree courses in:*

Polytechnics	yes/no **(circle one)**
Colleges of HE	yes/no **(circle one)**
Universities	yes/no **(circle one)**

5. *Is a discretionary grant available (ie. if your local authority so chooses) to mature students for PART-TIME degree courses in:*

Polytechnics   yes/no **(circle one)**
Colleges of HE   yes/no **(circle one)**
Universities   yes/no **(circle one)**

C. Nature of Courses

6. *What is the normal length of the following courses in England and Wales if taken on a FULL-TIME basis **(tick one number in each row)**.*

	1 year	2 years	3 years	4 years	5 years	6 years
Ordinary Degree						
Honours Degree						
HND						

7. *What is the normal length of the following courses in England and Wales if taken on a PART-TIME basis **(tick one number in each row)**.*

	2 years	3 years	4 years	5 years	6 years	7 years	8 years
Ordinary Degree							
Honours Degree							
HNC							

8. *Are degrees available in the following subjects at each type of institution **(add to each box a tick for "yes" or a cross for "no")**.*

	Universities	Polytechnics	Colleges of HE
Medicine			
Business Studies			
Textile Studies			
Engineering			
Philosophy			
English Literature			
Teacher Education			
Secretarial Studies			

D. Entrance Requirements

9. *What, in practice, are the minimum entry requirements for a mature student to enter higher education to study for a FULL-TIME degree **(tick one)**:*

a) No formal educational qualifications
b) 5 O-levels or equivalent

c) 1 A-level or equivalent
d) 2 A-levels or equivalent
e) 3 A-levels or equivalent

10. *What, in practice, are the minimum entry requirements for a mature student to enter higher education to study for a PART-TIME degree (tick one).*
   a) No formal educational qualifications
   b) 5 O-levels or equivalent
   c) 1 A-level or equivalent
   d) 2 A-levels or equivalent
   e) 3 A-levels or equivalent

E. Miscellaneous

11. *What percentage of FULL-TIME students in British higher education is mature (ie. aged 25 or more)? (circle one)*

   5% 8% 11% 14% 17% 20% 23% 26% 29% 32% 35% 38%

12. *What percentage of PART-TIME students in British higher education is mature (ie. aged 25 or more)? (circle one)*

   5% 10% 15% 20% 25% 30% 35% 40% 45% 50% 55% 60%

13. *The standard of degree achieved by mature students is, on average (tick one):*
   a) Significantly below that of those entering direct from school
   b) Slightly below that of those entering direct from school
   c) About the same as those entering direct from school
   d) Slightly better than those entering direct from school
   e) Significantly better than those entering direct from school

14. *Name three actual British institutions in each of the following categories:*

Universities ....

....

Polytechnics ....

....

Colleges of HE ....

....

15. *List your main sources of information about higher education, in order of priority (if none, say "none", and if you refer to any books, please give titles.)*

....

....

16. *What is your highest level of academic qualifications achieved* **(tick one)**:
    a) No formal qualifications
    b) O-levels or equivalent
    c) A-levels or equivalent
    d) Higher National Diploma or equivalent
    e) Degree

F. Possible Involvement in Higher Education

17. *On a scale of 1 to 5, are you at all likely to apply for a course in a university?* **(circle one number: 1 = not at all likely; 5 = extremely likely).**

    1   2   3   4   5

18. *On a scale of 1 to 5, are you at all likely to apply for a course in a polytechnic?* **(circle one number: 1 = not at all likely; 5 = extremely likely).**

    1   2   3   4   5

19. *On a scale of 1 to 5, are you confident of being able to find information about courses in higher education if you need it?* **(circle one number: 1= not at all confident; 5 = very confident).**

    1   2   3   4   5

20. *On a scale of 1 to 5, are you confident that you could, if you so wished, successfully complete a degree course?* **(circle one number: 1 = not at all confident; 5 = very confident).**

    1   2   3   4   5

21. *Indicate whether you are: Male / Female* **(circle one)**

Thank you for your help. Please return the questionnaire in the postage-paid envelope.

Appendix 3 Information about PCAS and its Publications

The Polytechnics Central Admissions System (PCAS) was established in 1984 to administer the process of applying to first degree and DipHE courses in all the polytechnics in England and Wales. The first students admitted through the system were enrolled in 1986. Since that date PCAS has expanded its services to include most of the colleges of higher education in England and Wales that offer degree courses and also the HND courses in all its constituent institutions. It has now extended its facilities to the Scottish Central Institutions.

PCAS believes that there is more to the applications process than simply an administrative bureaucracy. It has therefore developed a vigorous policy of advising all those connected with higher education entrance— applicants, their families, teachers, careers advisers and admissions tutors—so as to enable applicants and institutions alike to access all opportunities available to them in a fully informed manner. It underpins this with research and various consultancy activities.

It also offers day-long training packages for sixth-form teachers and careers officers on how to get the best out of admissions systems. All PCAS staff are encouraged to participate as fully as time allows in research, advisory, consultative and other activities which relate to matters of access to higher education.

PCAS Publications

As well as publishing statistical analyses on access to polytechnics and colleges, PCAS has also published (jointly with the Committee of Directors of Polytechnics, the Council for National Academic Awards, and the Centre for Educational Development and Training of Manchester Polytechnic) a study into the marketing to and admission of mature students, available from PCAS at £7.50 including post and packing:

Mature Students: Marketing and Admissions Policies

Introduction
Project aims; sample and methodology.

Chapter 1. Recruitment of Mature Students
The case for increased participation of mature students. The potential and current participation of mature students in higher education.

Chapter 2. Policy and Practice
Surveys of course leaders, admissions tutors and institutions' marketing personnel.

Chapter 3. Three Case Studies
Polytechnic of North London. Liverpool Polytechnic. Anglia Polytechnic.

Chapter 4. Summary Findings
Institutions' policy and practice. Mature students' background, experience and perceptions (drawn from surveys of current mature students and those mature students who had withdrawn from courses).

Chapter 5. Recommendations
Recommendations and a marketing strategy to enhance the recruitment of mature students, particularly in polytechnics and colleges, to full-time first-degree courses.

Other Publications

PCAS' other publishing activities include:

Video and teachers' pack *Crack the System* which is intended to brief potential applicants on their approach to applying to higher education. Available from PCAS on free loan.

A role-play game *The Application Game* which introduces school-leavers and others to the applications process in an enjoyable manner. Available from Hobsons Publishing plc, Bateman Street, Cambridge CB2 1LZ price £19.95.

Video and teacher's pack *A Two-Way Success* which advises on interview technique for applicants. Available from Trotman and Co Ltd, 12 Hill Rise, Richmond, Surrey TW10 6UA.

Update, a magazine for those in post-16 education in schools and colleges, distributed free each term.

A Mature Student's Guide to Higher Education, a booklet published annually (jointly with the Committee of Directors of Polytechnics) the current edition of which is incorporated in *Adults' Knowledge of Higher Education*. Available free from PCAS or CDP.

Appendix 4 Information about Heist and its Publications

Formed in 1987, Heist is a unique company which is concerned with marketing and public relations in higher and further education. Although financially independent, Heist is supported by PCAS, NATFHE, BTEC, CNAA and Leeds Polytechnic.

In addition to its research function, Heist also organises conferences and workshops and publishes books and magazines concerned with educational marketing. A range of consultancy services are also provided to individual institutions, ranging from prospectus editing and publications management, to market research and communications audits. Heist also provides a central distribution service for higher education prospectuses to schools and other centres throughout the UK and Europe.

Publications available from Heist include:

Young People's Knowledge of Higher Education (1990) by Keen and Higgins. Published by Heist/PCAS at £9.95 including postage and packing.

The full report of a survey involving over 7,000 sixth-form pupils in 691 schools/colleges which assessed the knowledge and perceptions of higher education amongst 'traditional' applicants.

The book will be of interest to careers advisers in schools, LEAs and colleges, and to those responsible for recruiting students in higher education including the editors of prospectuses and course leaflets.

'It is essential that we help our young people to make informed choices—and here is a valuable and readable book to identify the gaps that we need to fill. It would also come as a salutary reminder of gaps in our own knowledge.' (Newscheck with Careers Service Bulletin.)

Higher Education: The Student Experience (1992) by Roberts and Higgins. Published by Heist/PCAS at £14.95 including postage and packing.

This is a full report of a major survey—involving 5,650 students in over 100 higher education institutions—examining the views and experiences of students who had just completed one year of their undergraduate studies.

The research was undertaken by Heist, in association with PCAS, using three survey techniques: postal questionnaires, recorded focused discussion groups and semi-structured discussions in informal settings such as students' union bars and canteens.

The report covers four main areas: careers and educational guidance in schools, choosing institutions, the transition from sixth-form/college into higher education and the student as a consumer.

The book will be of interest and direct value to public relations and schools liaison staff in higher education, admissions tutors and counsellors and those advising sixth-formers on applying for higher education.

Public Relations Management in Colleges, Polytechnics and Universities (1988) by Keen and Greenall. Published by Heist at £10.95 including postage and packing.

This book covers the broader issues of public relations strategy, explaining both the nature and potential of professional public relations practice in the higher and further education environment.

'This book should be purchased by everyone who has the slightest interest in the promotion of their institution, be it a further or higher education college. . . .' (THES)

Visual and Corporate Identity (1989). Edited by Keen and Warner. Published by Heist at £9.95 including postage and packing.

A study of identity programmes in the college, polytechnic and university environments.

'Anyone interested in design and corporate identity will find this a most interesting collection of essays, covering every aspect of the subject. . . . This moderately priced book can be recommended to all in public relations.' (International Public Relations Review)

Promotional Publications: A Guide for Editors (1992) by Zoë Whitby. Published by Heist at £14.95 including postage and packing.

A comprehensive companion for editors working in all educational organisations who have responsibility for publications such as prospectuses, annual reports and course leaflets. The book covers project management, print, design and photography, sub-editing, sponsorship and advertising, publications research and much more.

Publications edited by Zoë Whitby have won awards for prospectuses, annual reports and course leaflets.

Promoting Education. A termly magazine published by Heist. Annual subscription £20 including postage and packing.

The magazine for public relations and marketing officers in further and higher education. Regular columns cover events and exhibitions, new reports and books, media update, the work of relevant support groups and the latest research.

Contributors include in-house practitioners, consultants and education journalists working throughout the UK and overseas.

Heist, The Grange, Beckett Park Campus, Leeds LS6 3QS
Tel. (0532) 833184

About the Authors

Clive Keen BA MA PhD MIPR

During the compilation of this book, Clive Keen was Professor of Public Relations Studies at Leeds Business School and Chief Executive of Heist. Just prior to its publication, he left Britain to become Director of External Relations of the newly created University of Northern British Columbia. He was previously responsible for public relations at Oxford Polytechnic, after spending a decade lecturing in Philosophy.

He has published a number of articles on both philosophy and public relations, and is author of *The College Prospectus*, co-author of *Public Relations Management* and *Young People's Knowledge of Higher Education*, and co-editor of *Visual and Corporate Identity*.

He has been a public relations consultant for a number of higher education institutions, and established two of the three undergraduate degree programmes in public relations in Britain.

His return to Canada has allowed allowed him to spend more time on the ski-slopes, and to develop his enthusiasm for caving in uncharted areas.

M A Higgins BA FBIM

Tony Higgins is the founding Chief Executive of the Polytechnics Central Admissions System (PCAS) and was instrumental in developing its approach to managing applications to higher education beyond simply the bureaucratic to ensuring that all potential applicants, their families and advisers are well prepared to make the best of their application.

He is co-author of *Young People's Knowledge of Higher Education*; *Higher Education: The Student Experience; Getting into Polytechnic;* and *How to Complete your UCCA/PCAS Form*. He has also broadcast, written for the press, and has contributed to a number of books and journals including *Higher Education Quarterly*, *Which Degree*, *The Adviser's Handbook*, *The Potter Guide to Higher Education*, and *Degree Course Offers*.

Prior to joining PCAS he was an administrator at Leicester and Loughborough Universities during which time he served a period as Chairman of the Conference of University Administrators.

In his spare time he is a member of the BBC Midlands and East of England Regional Advisory Council, President of the Haymarket Theatre, Leicester, Vice-Chairman of the Gloucestershire Everyman Theatre, and works on the Development Committee of the Cheltenham International Festivals of Music and Literature. He is also Chairman of Heist.